Putting on
PERFECT PROMS,
PROGRAMS,
& PAGEANTS

By Sallie G. Randolph

FRANKLIN WATTS
NEW YORK / LONDON / TORONTO / SYDNEY
1991

Photographs courtesy of: Ettore-Winter, Buffalo, N.Y.: pp. 12, 50 bottom, 79 bottom, 88, 103; National Archives: pp. 36, 78, 79 top; E. H. Butler Library, State University of New York, Buffalo: p. 50 top; Anderson's: pp. 57, 60, 63, 75, 117; Arcade Herald: pp. 112, 115; Mount Clemens High School, Michigan: p. 131.

Library of Congress Cataloging-in-Publication Data

Randolph, Sallie G.
Putting on perfect proms, programs, and pageants /
Sallie G. Randolph.
p.   cm.
Includes bibliographical references and index.
Summary: Describes how to plan a prom, program, or pageant
including budgets, committees and meetings, refreshments,
decorations, and publicity.
ISBN 0-531-11061-3
1. Balls (Parties)   2. Pageants.   [1. Balls (parties)
2. Pageants.]   I. Title.
GV1746.R36   1991
793.3'8—dc20   91-18527   CIP   AC

CONTENTS

For William E. Randolph II

ACKNOWLEDGMENTS

It would have been impossible to write this book without the generous help and information provided by students, teachers, administrators, librarians, researchers, and photographers across the country and the author gratefully recognizes their contributions.

Because many repeated the same sound advice and shared similar good ideas, their direct quotations have been paraphrased and sometimes attributed to composite individuals and examples. Likewise, the sample press releases and memoranda used in this book are based on composite examples. Examples and quotations, however, are based on suggestions and events from schools from all over the United States and Canada.

Many individuals gave generously of their time, wisdom, and experience and shared invaluable information, advice, and assistance. Some provided exceptional help and deserve to be acknowledged individually, including Suzanne Bissonette, Bonnie Randolph, Erin Harrington, Kathy Mason, Will Randolph, Douglas Sutherland, Amy Randolph, Dorothy D. Ennis, Budd Ennis, Dr. Vivian Stephens, Nancy

O'Keefe Bolick, Judy Morgenthall, Richard Randolph, Ronald E. Thompson, Carole Jones, Antoinette Michelle Crawford, Leanna Sturkey, Lola Hilton, Beth Buckley, John Romer, Kate E. Mabbette, Janet D. Vine, Susan Lambert, Alice Glazier, and David Weaver.

Pam Spencer and Reni Roxas contributed immeasurably by providing thoughtful evaluation, excellent suggestions, careful corrections, and skilled editing.

Help with photo research and photographs were provided by James Gavacs of Ettore-Winter Photographers, Buffalo, New York; Sister Martin Joseph Jones of the E.H. Butler Library, State University College of New York at Buffalo; Dale H. Connelly of the Still Picture Branch, National Archives of the United States, Washington, DC; Douglas Sutherland of Mount Clemens High School, Mount Clemens, Michigan; Kathleen L. Mason and Carole Jones of the Arcade *Herald*, Arcade, New York; Lola Hilton and John Romer of the Patuxent Air Naval Station, Maryland; and Paul Griffiths of Anderson's, White Bear Lake, Minnesota.

Special thanks, as always, go to John Randolph, who knows why.

1

PERFECT PROGRAMS = PEOPLE + PLANNING

Chris and Jessica had a great time at their senior prom in northern Virginia, even though it was held in the school gym over the strenuous objections of many students and some of their parents.

"I was really angry when the school board decided we had to have our prom in the gym," Jessica said. "I even went to a board meeting to speak out in favor of a hotel. I just couldn't imagine that the gym could be anywhere near as nice."

When the board of education held firm, though, students and faculty accepted the inevitable, put aside their disappointment, and pitched in to make the big night a success. The prom committee hired a New York City decorator to help teams of students transform the gym into a starry night in Venice. "It was spectacular," Jessica said. "I couldn't believe it."

"I helped with the decorations," Chris said. "We had a good time. I think I enjoyed myself at the prom more because I had a bigger stake in it. A hotel would have been okay, but you should have seen our Venice in the gym. We even built a big gondola."

When Ryan and Holly attended their senior prom

in an upstate New York community, they were both disappointed. Between them they spent more than $500 on tuxedo rental, dress, flowers, souvenir garter, limousine service, prom tickets, and entertainment after the prom. They had high expectations, but somehow the big night didn't live up to them. "I blew two months' savings on my share of the expenses," said Ryan. "I sure didn't have enough fun to justify that."

"It hurt our relationship, too," added Holly. "We were good friends and were dating casually. But so much seemed to be expected. I think it made us both feel pressure to make our relationship into something more than it was. We were never as comfortable with each other after prom night."

In some schools, a prom is an exciting rite of passage, a sparkling night filled with fun and fantasy. The students who participate in planning it have a rewarding experience and acquire skills that will serve them well as adults. The students who attend enjoy a pleasant introduction to formal, adult entertainment and take home meaningful souvenirs and cherished memories.

Sometimes, though, prom night is a major disappointment. Planning results in friction and hurt feelings. Students spend more than they can really afford. Some are left out completely because of the expense. Traditional rituals have disintegrated into commercialized excesses, and inflated expectations leave students feeling let down, even when the prom goes smoothly.

School festivals, programs, and pageants of all sorts can be satisfying to the students who plan them and interesting to everyone who attends. Or they can be marred by varying degrees of difficulty, problems, and friction.

What is it that makes some assemblies entertaining, informative, and interesting while the only redeeming feature of others is a break in the normal school schedule? Why are some homecoming pageants mechanical rituals while others are vibrant community celebrations? Why do some awards banquets grind on as guests dine on mediocre food and listen to long-winded speeches while other such dinners offer a memorable and enjoyable evening out? Why do some carnivals and festivals heighten awareness and raise large sums for worthy causes, while others have only a slight impact and barely make expenses?

PLANNING CHECKLIST

What makes the difference between great programs, good ones, so-so ones, and disappointing ones? Successful programs have certain common characteristics. The very best will have nearly all of them. Mediocre programs will have some, and poor programs will have few. Aim to inject as many of the vital features on the following list as possible into your school program. It should be:

Well-planned. Plan early, often a full year before the event. "Start as early as possible and delegate duty," says a junior class adviser in North Carolina who has helped plan many proms and school programs. "That's the single most important piece of advice I can offer."

Student-oriented. Involve as many participants as possible. Students should be well represented on committees and play an important role in the planning.

"Students have to be enthusiastic and their ideas have to receive serious consideration for an event to succeed," says a faculty adviser from a suburb of Washington, D.C. Efforts must be made to make the event satisfying for everyone expected to attend. The needs of all students and adults are considered. A few individuals or a particular clique should not dominate the planning.

In a good school program, the planners work well

*Good school programs are well-planned
and student-oriented.*

together. Adults provide guidance but allow students
to be leaders. Students from a broad cross-section of
the school population participate. Planning and partici-
pation allows for personal growth, fostering of respect
for others, the development of new friendships, and
strengthening of social skills.

Good school programs foster growth in the students who plan and attend them. They enhance positive social values and reinforce self-esteem. They
increase awareness, provide growth opportunities for
planners and participants, nurture respect for others,
and offer useful experience that can be applied to
adulthood.

Purposeful. Organizers and participants should
have clear goals and reasons for putting on a prom,

pageant, banquet, assembly, or award program. Everyone has realistic expectations. The program is meaningful to those who participate. People care about it. A single event might have several purposes. The primary reason for holding a freshman dance, for example, might be to offer a good time to those who attend. The dance also can be planned to raise funds for the class treasury and serve as an eye-opener to the students who later will be planning their prom.

Furthermore, good programs meet the purpose for which they were intended. The people who planned them have a sense of accomplishment, a feeling of a job well done.

This sense of satisfaction also means tying up loose ends. After the program, evaluations are made, thank yous are taken care of, recognition is arranged for, and cleanup is accomplished. Records, information, leftover supplies, notes, evaluations, and ideas are collected and saved for the next time.

Safe. Plan your school program in such a way that it includes plenty of opportunity for safe fun as well as incentives for students to stay clean and sober. Reasonable security precautions are taken and plenty of discreet adult supervision is available. Health department regulations, safety rules, and laws are carefully complied with. Good planners use plenty of common sense and caution.

Creative. Be open to fresh ideas and new approaches within the framework of rules and traditions. Students are given opportunities to use their talents and abilities. Early brainstorming is encouraged. All ideas, whether they are used or not, are treated with respect. There is recognition that any idea, no matter how silly, half-baked, or inappropriate it may seem, can lead to another and that creativity can only flourish in an atmosphere of openness, trust, and respect.

Appropriate. Be faithful to the purpose you've se-

13

lected for your event. Serious events are dignified, although humor can be used to lighten up even the most sombre occasion. Pep assemblies are designed to generate enthusiasm. Ceremonies are rich with tradition. Dances and parties are festive and fun.

Participants in all types of school events dress and act according to the dictates of tradition and propriety. Decorations, theme, menu, entertainment, agenda, and site are carefully selected with the type of occasion in mind.

Practical. Exercise creativity, but be realistic about your expectations and find ways to make your ideas work within the limitations of school rules, budgets, and time frames. A spirit of compromise and willingness to adapt are essential. Programs make economic sense and have realistic budgets. Those who pay to attend receive honest value for their dollars. Efforts are made to keep costs reasonable and programs affordable for the students who attend. Funds are raised, handled, and expended with great care. Spending is evaluated in the light of program goals. Budget decisions are prioritized on an ongoing basis.

Not all good school programs will have every one of these characteristics, but most successful programs will have many of these vital qualities. Keep them in mind as you plan.

PLANNING PAYS

Students at a high school in northern New Jersey were bitterly disappointed when they started to plan for their June prom in September and learned that the best facilities were already booked through every weekend in May and June. Finally, they were forced to hold their prom in April at a third-choice location.

The homecoming parade in a rural Arkansas community never came off because of a schedule mix-up. The sheriff's department closed off Main Street and spectators gathered on Friday evening, but no bands or floats showed up. Parade units had been mistakenly informed to gather at the staging area on Saturday afternoon. Since the homecoming game was scheduled for Saturday evening, everyone assumed that the parade would take place immediately before the game and no one questioned the misprint.

The annual senior recognition ceremony at a high school in Michigan ended abruptly due to lack of time. To the acute disappointment of their recipients, several awards had not yet been presented when classes were scheduled to resume. Earlier, speeches of gratitude had been allowed to continue for too long because no one had prepared a timed agenda or conducted a trial run through the program ahead of time.

A chicken barbecue arranged by a junior class in Ohio as a charity fund-raiser was shut down by the county health department because students had used refrigeration methods that violated county health regulations.

Kathy and Jessica, lifelong friends from Connecticut, had a terrible fight over who was supposed to have handled which detail for the swim-a-thon they were organizing to raise money for the Red Cross. The swim-a-thon was ultimately a success, but the friendship was seriously jeopardized.

These disappointments were preventable through planning. Planning isn't hard if you keep five important guidelines in mind.

Begin Early. The preliminary planning for a recurring, traditional event, such as a prom, might start several *years* ahead of time. In some school districts, the freshman class begins fund-raising for its senior prom and sets the date by the beginning of the sophomore year. Whether you are planning a major event or a small meeting, starting as soon as you reasonably can makes sense.

Look to the Past. Gather all the information that is available about past events. Ask previous organizers. Look for notes, lists, bills, schedules, and old programs. Find out as much as you possibly can about previous programs. This will help you to duplicate successes, avoid problems, and find sources of help and supplies.

"The most useful thing I had to work with was the previous adviser's notebook, which she passed on to me," says a junior class adviser from North Carolina. "She kept track of all the phone calls she made, the people she recruited, the suppliers she ordered from, the locations that were considered, and the notes of the meetings. That notebook was a gold mine."

Look to the Future. Envision what you want the program to be like. Use your imagination to make a mental journey through the event. Think about what it will take to make everything perfect and begin working toward that goal. Not everything will go exactly as you envision it, of course, but having a clear goal will help the planning.

Put Your Plans in Writing. Make written lists. Keep track of decisions made at meetings. Post dates ahead of time. Follow up with memos that keep the people involved fully informed. Keep a notebook. Written records make communication clearer, mistakes less likely, and planning more efficient. This doesn't mean you have to labor over an extensive document or write everything in a rigid formal way. Written plans can be as simple as a brief list, a short note, a quick memo, or a bulletin board item. Jotting down is writing. Shopping lists, notebooks, assignment sheets, budget worksheets, decorating charts, and committee assignment rosters are all examples of written plans.

Stay Flexible. Planning is a process that continues

until the event is completely wrapped up. It involves continuous adjustment, fine-tuning, and polishing.

"A lot of people forget that planning continues right up until the moment of the big night and beyond," says a faculty adviser from Alabama. "It's a big mistake to think that plans are made first and then engraved in stone. You have to be flexible and able to adapt. Things are changing all the time. A good planner makes change work out for the best."

PEOPLE MAKE PLANS

When the committee selected her as chair of the prom, Amanda was delighted. She had lots of ideas and was ready to put them into action. But Mrs. Kennedy, the class adviser, had been planning proms for many years and insisted on doing everything. At first Amanda tried to contribute, but Mrs. Kennedy politely ignored all of her suggestions and just went ahead making arrangements. Amanda gave up. She attended the prom. People seemed to have a good time. Amanda did, too, but the evening lacked the extra sparkle she'd been looking forward to.

Even the best-planned and perfectly executed event is a failure if it results in stress, negative feelings, tension, or frustration. And a slapdash, haphazardly planned event where people nonetheless have a good time and the work somehow gets done because everyone pitches in is still a success. It's important to remember that people—how they work together, feel about each other, and feel about themselves—are what any school activity is all about.

A major school event such as a pageant, carnival, festival, or prom brings together many people, both students and adults, who must work effectively together, sometimes under tense conditions. This can be an opportunity to make new friends and function as part of a winning team. But if the people involved harbor negative attitudes, the results can be devastating.

"My best friend and I signed up to work on decorations for our senior prom," recalls Sarah, a Minnesota senior. "I thought we'd have a good time, but we couldn't agree on anything and we ended up having a big fight. Although we both made an effort to patch things up, our friendship has never really been as close."

A New England senior had a better experience working on a committee. "My family moved to Vermont in the middle of my sophomore year. I didn't know anyone and this is a pretty tight rural community. I signed on to work on my junior prom and got to know a few kids. Then I worked on the homecoming committee in the fall of my senior year. By then I'd made new friends and even got a part-time job with one of the local business owners I met while I was out selling ads for the program. Working on school events is a good way to meet people and gain acceptance."

There are four essential keys to working well with other people.

Understand Goals. Why do you want to work on this program or that committee? What are the motives of the others working with you? Maybe you want to gain leadership experience that will look good on a college application. Perhaps you want the event to be fun and you think you have some good ideas. You might want to get out of babysitting for your little brother and serving on a particular committee offers you a good excuse. Are you interested in getting to know another person working on the same project? Have you been pressured into joining by a parent, teacher, or friend? Is there a specific thing, such as decorating, that you particularly enjoy?

Understanding your own motives as well as the

motives of others will help you respond more appropriately when problems come up.

Thinking about the reasons why you want to be involved will sharpen your perspective. If you realize that you're not that enthusiastic about the project and that you're really just humoring a friend, you can comfortably afford to let him or her take more of a leadership role. Not only will your support be appreciated by your friend but it will make you feel good. By understanding your own role a little better, you'll be more patient and willing to play second fiddle to your friend.

Understanding your own motives can help you avoid becoming overcommitted, too. It can keep your stress level more manageable. Know your strengths and limitations. Don't kid yourself. Know when to say no. And clarify what you mean when you say yes. Resist the temptation to make excuses, to cover up, or to agree to do something you don't really think you can. Sometimes it's hard to be honest about your goals, yet honesty both with yourself and with others can save you a lot of trouble.

Understand Roles. All school events will need a leader, someone in charge who coordinates the efforts of everyone involved. This leader, most often called the chairman or chair, could also be the director, coordinator, senior adviser, or president.

Depending on their size and scope, events will also require an assistant to the leader, heads of major committees, committee members, adult advisers, volunteer workers, vendors of goods and services, and paid workers. All of these people must work together effectively by filling their roles appropriately in order to produce a winning event.

The role of the leader is often misunderstood. His or her most important skill is that of delegating. If the leader makes all decisions and does all the work, the results will not be as good as when the leader confers, consults, and delegates. A good leader recruits strong people, motivates them to do their jobs, coordinates their efforts, and follows up with guidance, insight, and advice. A good leader is enthusiastic, open to ideas, persuasive, a good listener, and able to delegate authority and jobs.

A follower agrees to provide his or her ideas, expertise, labor, and effort. A good follower understands the roles of everyone on the committee or group and understands exactly what is expected in the job he or she has agreed to do. It's fine for a committee member to contribute his or her own ideas, but not at the expense of meddling in the jobs of others. The follower understands the scope of the individual job, does it, and reports back to the leader. A good follower must be a willing worker, one who can take advice and direction. A follower knows how to make suggestions but is also prepared to carry out the instructions of others.

Some people will be both leaders and followers. The chair of the decorations committee, for example, will report to the general chair and will carry out decisions that have already been made about theme, budget, and time. But the decoration chair will lead a large group of committee members, volunteers, and paid professionals in the actual decorating and will make many important decisions. Working as a subcommittee chair is a good way to gain valuable leadership experience and sharpen following skills as well.

There is one other role that is important to understand and, if necessary, to clarify with everyone involved. The faculty adviser or school administrator assigned to supervise student planning of events can be a vital source of guidance, inspiration, and help. Sometimes the adviser functions more like a chair, with specific authority and responsibilities. In many cases the adviser or other adult must supervise students in such areas as negotiations with outside vendors. But the adviser's most important role is to help students do a good job. A good adviser gives advice, help, encouragement, suggestions, and information—not orders. And student leaders respect the experience and wisdom of their advisers.

Student leaders and advisers should sit down early in the planning process and agree on appropriate roles for everyone to follow, then put each person's duties and responsibilities in writing. If everyone understands their roles, people will work more smoothly together.

Communicate Clearly. The single most important communication skill is listening. Concentrate on what others are saying. Respect their ideas. If you're not sure what they mean, request clarification. Make sure you understand what is expected by the others. Listening carefully is the single most effective thing you can do to avoid misunderstanding.

Sarah, the Minnesota senior whose friendship with Kelly, another student, was jeopardized while planning decorations for their senior prom, blames a failure to listen as a major source of friction. "We each had strong opinions about how we should decorate the gym. I didn't really want to hear what Kelly thought and I know she didn't want to hear my ideas. I guess I expected to be in charge and that Kelly would be my willing assistant. It's sad, because if we had listened to each other we could probably have come up with fresh ideas. Instead we argued."

Just because you listen carefully to someone else's ideas and respect his or her opinion doesn't mean you have to agree. But if you have taken the trouble to understand the other point of view, consider it, and respond in a thoughtful way, your own opinion will count more with others. If you are not sure what is expected of you, be sure to ask. Likewise, make sure you tell others what you expect of them. As the planning process moves along, repeat the clarification process. Communication is asking, telling, clarifying, and listening. Keep the lines of communication open.

Related communication skills include diplomacy and courtesy. Diplomacy is the ability to convey information, give orders, and handle difficult situations in a way that results in the best outcome for the most people, with the fewest hurt feelings and unpleasant encounters along the way. Diplomacy is the ability to be honest in a positive way. For example, instead of saying, "That's a terrible idea," when you think it is, try saying "That's an imaginative idea, but I wonder if it will work well in this particular situation."

Being courteous to others shows that you respect and appreciate their feelings. If you try to remain courteous and polite no matter how provoked or how frustrated you feel, you'll get a lot farther in your dealings with people than if you give in to the temptation to snap at them, order them around, gossip about them, or lose your temper. Being courteous sometimes means taking the necessary time to disengage or stop, think, and regain control of your temper. Sometimes the courteous thing to do is to put off a discussion until everyone has had a chance to think and cool off. Formal etiquette is merely ritualized courtesy, the following of ground rules that you treat others with courtesy and in turn are yourself treated courteously.

Demonstrating respect for others is another vital communication skill. Respect the rights, ideas, and feelings of others and, most of all, respect yourself. If you follow the golden rule and treat others with the same respect you expect them to show for you, you'll communicate effectively. Keep in mind that respect doesn't necessarily mean agreement. You can respectfully decline a suggestion or respectfully disagree. But when a decision is made or a person who has authority over you makes a suggestion, you can comply out of respect. Confidence grows with self-respect, and self-respect grows with respect for others.

Separate Principles from Personalities. "I was astonished to discover that I could work well with people that I didn't even like," one student says. It pays to put aside personal animosity, social delineations, resentments, and differences and to concentrate instead on mutual goals. Your committee should be neutral, your event open to all segments of the student body. Work should focus on carrying out responsibilities and on achieving results, not on personalities and differences between people.

Amanda and Mrs. Kennedy both could have had a more satisfying experience planning the senior prom if they had understood their roles and communicated more clearly. Better communication and better understanding of roles would have helped the Minnesota senior whose friendship was damaged, too. The Vermont student used his people skills to make new friends and adapt to a new community. You too can avoid or solve most people problems by making sure that you:

- Understand goals.
- Understand roles.
- Communicate clearly.
- Separate principles from personalities.

PLANNING FOR PROBLEMS

There's a humorous law that says, "Whatever can go wrong, will." That's certainly true of school programs. No matter how well you plan, how carefully organized you are, and how hard you work, problems are sure to crop up.

Just as you must plan for such things as decorations, food, and entertainment, you must plan for trouble, too. Planning for problems is the first step in preventing them. And the ones you can't prevent can be solved with a minimum of fuss if you've thought about how you'd handle difficult situations.

Fortunately, most troubles are not serious ones, and most problems are not insurmountable. You'll deal with the smaller trials and tribulations more easily when you're prepared and when you recognize that, contrary to the title of this book, there's no such thing as a perfect program. It's okay to aim for perfection as long as you can accept that you're going to have to settle for something less. Ironically, sometimes the less you settle for, the more you end up enjoying.

Common sense, realistic expectations, and self-confidence will serve you well most of the time, so don't let trouble spoil your good time. Think back to some of your happiest school memories. Chances are they're related to funny situations that arose out of problems or glitches. Remember that it's not how well you manage to eliminate problems but how well you deal with the results of them that counts. Sometimes the best way to deal with a problem is to solve it. Other times the best choice will be to accept the situation and overlook it. It helps to keep your perspective, keep your cool, and use your sense of humor to help you through.

2
ORGANIZING FOR SUCCESS

The process of organizing a school event can be broken down into a series of logical steps. The early steps include getting interested planners together, setting a date, gathering information, and establishing a timetable. The sequence of these first steps depends on a variety of factors. Sometimes an organizational structure is already in place. The date might have been included on a school-year calendar.

Planners should start with what they have, assess the situation, and go from there, using the three basic organizational tools: *lists, meetings,* and *committees.* Getting organized means making an overall list of the major things that need to be accomplished. Then the things on the list are sorted into categories. These categories become the nucleus of an organizational structure.

PLANNING TOOLS

Lists are what planners make dozens of during the preparation process—lists of ideas, lists of tasks that need to be done, lists of people to carry out the tasks, lists of ideas to consider, lists of problems to be solved, lists of supplies to obtain, and lists of schedules. Planning lists evolve into notebooks, timetables, schedules, agendas, organizational charts, committee rosters, brainstorming sessions, and budgets.

Meetings are where people get together to work with lists and make decisions. At meetings, lists become the basis for gathering information, making decisions, assigning tasks, and turning ideas into activity and achievements. Meetings are most effective if they are well organized, regularly scheduled, reasonably brief, follow an agenda, and are announced far enough in advance that most key people are able to attend.

One person, usually the chair, should run a meeting and someone else, appointed by the chair, should write down all major things that have been discussed and decided upon. These notes should then be typed, copied, and distributed to all committee members.

A plan, or agenda for the meeting, should be decided on ahead of time. Usually, this is the responsibility of the chair or adult adviser. Participants should be notified of both the date and time of the meeting and the proposed agenda. Those who wish to raise subjects for discussion should contact the meeting leader ahead of time and ask to be put on the agenda. Two types of sample agendas, one with a timetable and the other more informal, follow:

SAMPLE TIMED AGENDA

MEMORANDUM
TO: Senior Awards Assembly Committee Members

FROM: Andrea Chan, Chair
       Senior Awards Assembly Committee

SUBJECT: Agenda for October 3 meeting

3:30 pm   Introduction of committee
3:40 pm   Selections of date for Awards Assembly
3:50 pm   Discussion of awards to be presented and time
          allotted
4:20 pm   Tentative agenda prepared for Awards Assembly

4:45 pm   "Walk-through" of program, delegate responsi-
          bilities
5:00 pm   Adjournment

SAMPLE MEMO AND AGENDA

DATE: September 5, 1991

TO: All Prom Committee Members,
      Subcommittee Chairs,
      Principal,
      Class Advisers

FROM: Pam Roland, General Chair

SUBJECT: Next Meeting/Pine Valley Prom Steering Com-
           mittee

The next meeting will be held on Monday, Sept. 16, right after school in Room 112. As you know, our planning is
getting into high gear and we have a lot to accomplish, so
we'll try to stick as closely as possible to this agenda:

1. Committee reports
2. Final selection of theme from these choices:
   "Magic of the Night"
   "A Little Night Music"
   "Starry Night in Centerville"
   "The Night Belongs to You and Me"
   "A Night to Remember"
3. Discussion and adoption of budget
4. Scheduling of and setting preliminary agenda for
   next meeting.

This will probably make for a pretty full meeting, but if you
have any other items you would like added to the agenda,
put your request in writing and send it to me care of Mrs.
Wynaski in Room 112 by Thursday, Sept. 12, at 3:00 pm.

Thanks. I'll look forward to seeing you all.

Pam Roland

At the beginning of the meeting the leader should introduce everyone present, explain the purpose of the meeting, and pass out written agendas or verbally list things to be covered. The leader will moderate discussion and conduct any necessary votes. At the end of the meeting the chair should summarize what has been decided and accomplished. The chair should also announce the time, date, and agenda of the next meeting. After the meeting a summary should be sent to everyone involved (see sample minutes on page 29).

"Sticking to the agenda is sometimes hard, but it's really important," says an experienced committee chair. "You can waste hours on meaningless discussion by getting sidetracked."

Committees form the basis for the most common and convenient planning structure for most school programs. The number, size, and function of committees will depend on the event. A major undertaking such as a prom or festival will have a nucleus of leaders who form some sort of supervisory organization. This might be called a steering committee, central committee, management group, executive committee, or just plain committee.

When the core leadership has identified the major areas of responsibility and selected an overall leader, usually called the chairman or chair, various subcommittees are established, each chaired by someone who is responsible for implementation of certain items on the list of jobs to be done. New committees or subcommittees can be created as need dictates.

Many times, the preliminary organizers form a temporary structure that allows planning to get under way at the same time as volunteers are recruited. A temporary chair will later be replaced by a permanent one and the preliminary committee will evolve as jobs are identified and filled. Such a temporary structure is

SAMPLE MINUTES

DATE: September 13, 1991

TO: All Prom Committee Members,
Subcommittee Chairs,
Principal,
Class Advisers

FROM: Pam Roland, General Chair

SUBJECT: Summary of September 12 Meeting

Our last planning meeting went well. All committees reported progress as planned, except for the decorating committee, which was waiting for the selection of the theme to proceed.

"A Little Night Music" was unanimously chosen as our theme.

A total preliminary budget of $12,000 was adopted, with the principal's and adviser's approval. This is $1,200 more than last year. Some committee budgets will need to be cut to accommodate this figure and ticket prices will be $12.50 per student with an expected paid attendance of 500 students and guests. This budget represents a compromise between our "dream plans" and what is affordable. $3,200 has already been raised or pledged for the prom, leaving about $2,550 to be raised by June. Planned fund-raising activities include bake sales; the annual "Litter Pick-Up" where our class is paid by Merchants' Association for each bag of trash we collect for recycling; the Holiday Ball; the Varsity/Faculty Basketball Game and sales of hot chocolate and popcorn at our class booth in the Community Winter Festival. Additional fund-raising ideas are welcome.

The next meeting is scheduled for October 19, same time, same place. We plan to discuss decorations, music, and the evening's program as well as any items that come up in the meantime. Please contact me if there are any items you would like placed on the agenda.

Best,

Pam Roland

often referred to as *pro tem*, a Latin term which means for the time being.

Exactly what committees you will use will depend on the needs of your group and the scope of your event. Some types of committees are used by almost every type of event. Others are specifically adapted for a particular event.

COMMON COMMITTEES

Some of the most typical committees include the following:

Decorations. Members of this vital committee participate in the planning of a theme; study and measure the area to be decorated; plan the decorations, incorporating the theme, if there is one, and make floor plans or charts as necessary. The committee also makes an inventory of decorating supplies and equipment on hand; establishes a decorating budget to work within and gets budget approval by the financial committee; buys, borrows, and finds decorating materials; builds or constructs sets and props; puts up the decorations before the event; helps clean up after the event; inventories and arranges for storage of reusable equipment and supplies.

Finance. This committee gathers financial information and organizes it into a budget; keeps track of money and expenditures and reports regularly as planning progresses; finds out required school procedures for handling cash, accounting, and record keeping. The finance committee will work with established school accounts and procedures or may set up special bank accounts and money-handling methods. Most schools have stringent regulations for handling funds, so the first task of the finance chair should be to meet with the principal or school business manager to work out procedures and guidelines. This is an area where adult help is especially important.

Arrangements. This committee is in charge of selecting a site, making appropriate reservations, and coordinating on-site activities such as decorating, delivery of supplies, allocation of space, and other physical arrangements.

Entertainment. This committee, sometimes called the activities or program committee, makes plans for and schedules speakers, master of ceremonies, special dances, grand march, coronation of king and queen, games and activities, and other entertainment or program elements of the event.

Music. The music committee decides on the type of music that will be provided, then lines up and negotiates with bands, sound systems, and other providers of music services. The music committee may be involved with the selection of a theme and with planning the program schedule.

Prize. The prize committee buys prizes or solicits donations of prizes, gets the prizes gathered before the event and distributed in a fair and appropriate way. This committee keeps track of all prizes and their value, makes sure any displayed prizes are securely watched and follows up with appropriate thank yous.

Publicity. This committee makes a publicity plan and prepares and distributes posters, press releases, television and radio announcements, and letters as necessary to parents, teachers, students, and community leaders. It may also plan special promotional events.

Tickets. The ticket committee establishes ticket prices in conjunction with the finance committee, arranges for the printing and distribution of tickets, keeps track of ticket sales, and reports regularly on progress.

Other Committees. These may or may not be necessary and include security, fund-raising, photography, advertising, programs, cleanup, and community relations. You may need different committees for your event or you may choose to combine committee responsibilities into different patterns. The prom-arrangements committee, for example, might handle photography, music, and printed programs at one school, while these things are the responsibility of different committees at another school. The important thing is to make sure every committee's responsibilities are clearly defined and understood by everyone. Committees are task and function oriented. In other words, when a job that needs to be done is identified, a committee is created to take care of it or the job is assigned to an already existing committee. Some committees are large and complex, but it is perfectly OK for a committee to be one or two people.

A sample organizational committee chart for a prom event is provided on pages 34 and 35.

GETTING THE STRUCTURE IN PLACE

Lining up Leaders. Once the date of an event has been set, its scope established, and a preliminary organizational structure agreed upon, recruiting of students and adults to fill leadership positions should begin. "Don't line up all the leaders too early, though," warns one experienced teacher. "Save some slots to be filled later as kids hear about what's going on and enthusiasm spreads. If the leadership is locked in right away, many students won't bother to get involved."

For major events such as festivals, carnivals, homecomings, pageants, and proms, planners should meet regularly with their efforts coordinated by an overall chairperson. At first the chairperson's job will be to identify things that need to be done, run meetings, solicit ideas, keep track of what's been decided, and find appropriate people to head committees.

Making Decisions. Every step of the process involves making decisions. Many decisions will be made informally, by consensus. Some will be made by school officials. A few will be dictated by school policy, rules, and regulations. Others will be made after voting or other more formal ways of reaching agreement. Many will be delegated to the appropriate committees or co-chairs.

Some decisions will be controversial or difficult to reach. Others will be easy to make. The group should agree on the ground rules of the decision-making process. These rules can cover such things as time limits for debate and discussion and whether decisions will be made by consensus (unanimous agreement), a simple majority, or individual decision of the chair once the discussion is complete. It is vital that the chair keep track of what has been decided already and what remains to be decided, and then to be sure everyone involved is informed. Clear communication during the decision-making process will make things run far more smoothly.

Key decisions should be made early. Some things that need to be discussed and decided upon include the date, location, scope, theme, budget, and goals of an event. It helps to focus on one major decision at a time in a logical sequence. And it's important to delegate decision-making when appropriate. Everything doesn't have to be voted on or decided by everybody. It makes more sense to decide on the people who will make decisions and then let those people carry on from there. This is delegation of duty and it's a good way to save time, energy, and frustration.

Holding Meetings. As the planning process continues, meetings become important steps along the way to success. Once the framework is in place, leaders have been recruited, and regular meetings are under way, progress can be smooth, with the likelihood of mistakes reduced to a minimum by keeping the lines of communication open and getting together regularly.

During its first meeting, each committee should

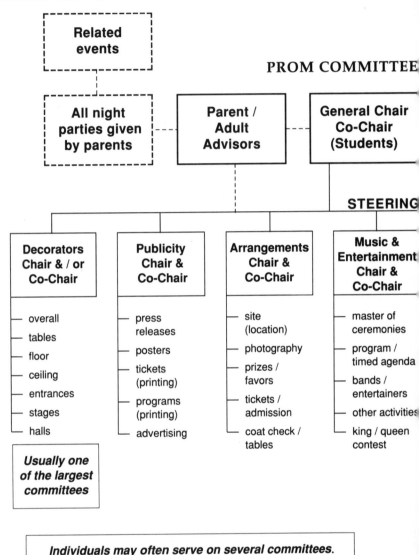

PROM COMMITTEE

Related events

All night parties given by parents

Parent / Adult Advisors

General Chair Co-Chair (Students)

STEERING

Decorators Chair & / or Co-Chair
- overall
- tables
- floor
- ceiling
- entrances
- stages
- halls

Usually one of the largest committees

Publicity Chair & Co-Chair
- press releases
- posters
- tickets (printing)
- programs (printing)
- advertising

Arrangements Chair & Co-Chair
- site (location)
- photography
- prizes / favors
- tickets / admission
- coat check / tables

Music & Entertainment Chair & Co-Chair
- master of ceremonies
- program / timed agenda
- bands / entertainers
- other activities
- king / queen contest

Individuals may often serve on several committees.

ORGANIZATIONAL CHART

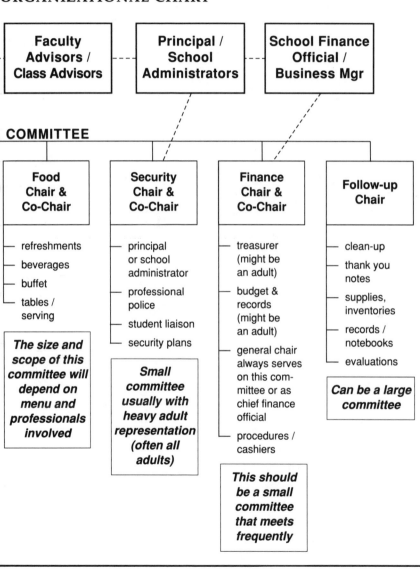

*Counselors and teachers can help guide students
in putting together a school event.*

discuss and clarify its goals and responsibilities, name
a chair (if this hasn't been done already), and establish
a timetable of tasks that need to be done and their
deadlines. Subsequent meetings will be used to keep
track of progress, deal with any problems that come up,
make intermediate decisions, and do the necessary
work to keep the planning moving along the steps to a
successful event. After each meeting, a brief report
should be prepared and sent to all members.

Following Up. Perhaps you will be surprised to
learn that planning for an event continues even after the
event is over. An integral step in the planning process,
and an important source of information is evaluation. It

will help planning for the next time if each program is carefully evaluated, in writing if possible, and certainly by discussion, by participants and planners. Evaluation rounds out the process, tying up the ends of one event at the same time it starts the cycle all over again.

The physical cleanup after your event is important, too, and must be planned for. Wrapping up of various loose ends, making final committee reports, making sure that thank-you notes get written, borrowed and rented items are returned, supplies and equipment are inventoried and put away are all vital tasks that are too often overlooked. Be sure to schedule a follow-up meeting to evaluate the program and make final reports, and make sure that all follow-up details have been taken care of.

"It's easy to overlook important details when the party is over," says an adviser. "It's a good idea to appoint a special person whose sole job it is to make sure that all those small but important things, such as the writing of thank-you notes, get done. In our school we have a special Mop-up Committee and its chair is the first one appointed. It's smart to start out with the ending."

3
MONEY MATTERS

"When we held our athletic dinner at a local restaurant we decided to have punch and coffee before and afterward," says the Varsity Club adviser at a New England high school. "The restaurant quoted us a price of $8.95 per meal, including the tax and service charge. We added a little bit for decorations and charged $10 for tickets to the dinner. We figured that we'd come out ahead and have some funds left over for the scholarship fund. The dinner was great and everyone had a fine time. People hung around to talk afterward. The restaurant kept refilling the punch bowl. What we didn't realize was that they were charging us by the gallon. When it was time to pay the bill we were over budget by more than $500. We had to have a special fund-raiser just to pay for all that punch."

Caroline was in charge of her prom decorating committee. When she ran out of crepe paper in mid-afternoon she asked the faculty adviser for some cash to get more.

"Take twenty dollars from the box," the adviser told Caroline. She did and headed for the store. She returned with the crepe paper and change. When she went to put the receipt and change back in the box she discovered it empty.

"It wasn't a lot of money missing, thank God," said Caroline. "But the incident cast a shadow over the prom for me. I wondered if anyone suspected me of taking the money. And I wondered which of my friends could have done it. It was awful."

PLANNING WELL

Whether you're trying to raise funds for a worthy cause, organize a theme festival, hold an assembly program, or put on a memorable dance, your planning will almost certainly involve money in one way or another. And money has to be dealt with carefully. Planning will help you avoid unpleasant financial surprises and money problems.

Learning the Rules. "If there's ever any one area in a school where teachers and students could get in serious trouble, it's with mismanagement of funds," notes an experienced adviser. "Many school systems have very complicated and stringent rules for handling money. It's always a good idea for a student finance officer, treasurer, or financial adviser to meet with everyone involved with money to explain the rules."

Establishing a Budget. Almost every event, no matter how modest, will have some direct costs associated with it. Those costs have to be planned for by establishing a budget. A budget is simply a plan. You establish a budget by figuring out exactly what funds will be available to you and then how they will be spent or allocated.

Start by gathering information on how much your event will cost to put on. Ask each committee to make as complete a list of supplies and materials as possible. Canvass price quotes from vendors of goods and services. If you're planning to hold your prom in a hotel, for example, make sure you understand exactly how the hotel will break down the charges and whether it charges by the person or by quantity, or charges a flat rate, or a combination. Ask about taxes, gratuities, and other extra items that could be added to the final bill.

Be as detailed as possible. If necessary, call and obtain comparative prices from other suppliers in order to arrive at a reasonable range. Gather as many records from past events as possible to find out what expenses were incurred then. Collect as much information as you can. Facts and figures will allow you to develop a working financial plan that holds few unpleasant surprises.

Once you've gathered all the necessary information, you can begin to prepare a budget. The preliminary budget will be a "wish list" of everything planners would like to include in the event. Each committee should make a detailed list of all the materials it will need to carry out its assigned functions (see sample budget request form below). Then costs in the lists should be added up to come up with an overall figure.

COMMITTEE BUDGET REQUEST FORM

Name of Committee: Publicity
Committee Chair: Anita Velasquez

Expenses (Itemize)	Actual/ Last Year	Projected/ This Year
postage	$25.00	$25.00
supplies for posters & banners	$25.00	$40.00
	TOTAL Expenses	$65.00

Now it's time to figure out where the money will come from to pay for all the proposed expenses. A class that has been raising prom funds for several years, for example, might have a sizable chunk of the budget already available. The prom treasurer or financial chair should begin by listing all the funds on hand. Next should be a list of sources of money that planners can reasonably expect to obtain. Revenue from program advertising, commissions from contract photographers, contributions from businesses and community groups, and other expected funds would be listed here.

A simplified sample budget worksheet is provided below.

OVERALL BUDGET WORKSHEET

	Actual/ Last Year	Projected/ This Year
Expenses		
Decorations	2,300	1,000
Ballroom Rental/Hotel	3,500	4,000
Refreshments	2,000	3,000
Souvenirs/Gifts/		
Programs	1,500	2,000
Other & Contingency	1,500	2,000
TOTAL	10,800	12,000
Funding Sources		
Money on hand		
(previously raised)		3,200
To be raised or donated		2,250
		5,450
TOTAL	$10,800	$12,000

NUMBER ATTENDING   500
EXPENSES PER PERSON   24.00
INCOME PER PERSON $11.00 (10.90)
ADDITIONAL AMOUNT TO BE RAISED PER PERSON
                (Basis for Ticket Price) $13.00

Use this worksheet as a starting point. Customize your budget worksheet to meet the specific needs of your event.

When the income from all sources has been projected, the difference between the total projected expenses and total projected income will be calculated. This difference will be the amount of additional money that needs to be raised from ticket sales or other funding or, if the organizers are lucky, the leftover amount that they can spend on extras. Setting ticket prices for events is a tricky process. Don't be discouraged if your early efforts result in extremely high projected prices. You now have a starting point. Now you'll have to start the process of adapting wishes to reality.

Making Choices and Setting Priorities. Now comes some decision-making. If the proposed expenses for your prom mean that the charge per ticket will have to be $70, organizers will probably prefer to cut expenses. Each committee will now be asked to cut its requests by a certain percentage until expenses and income are reasonably aligned.

Planners will also have to project attendance in order to arrive at a reasonable budget figure. Costs for some items will be per person, but other costs will be fixed, regardless of the number of people who attend.

Handling Funds. Even on a small subcommittee, there should be at least two people with control over funds, and committees should have carefully thought out procedures for handling cash, even modest amounts. If large amounts are involved, it will be vital to arrange for adult supervision and compliance with school regulations. The treasurer and/or finance committee chair should make a point of learning the mechanics of handling money by asking the faculty adviser, school office personnel, and previous treasurers how things are done. Any cash, even small amounts, should be watched at all times.

If your group is selling tickets or items at a fair or carnival, make sure the people handling the cash know how to make change and fill out receipts. Be sure there is plenty of change on hand at the beginning of the day. It's a good idea to practice change-making and cash-handling techniques before the event.

"When we decided to have our popcorn booth at the winter carnival, we asked a business teacher to help us plan the way we would handle money," says a student. "We practiced ahead of time so that things would go smoothly."

"Don't let amounts of cash build up or sit around," advises a store manager who often helps student groups prepare for ticket sales. "Have someone take cash inside to a safe place or to the bank at regular intervals. And, of course, it goes without saying that cash should be watched every second. It's a good idea to have someone stand near the booth or table and simply watch the money box. That person should have no other responsibilities so he or she can't be easily distracted. Cash watch duty should be rotated fairly often, too, at least once an hour, so the watchers don't become bored and inattentive."

Funds on hand should be counted frequently, with the amount checked and verified by a second person. Storing and transferring very large amounts of money need to be handled with extra care. Sometimes the local police department will provide an escort service to the bank. Some organizations even hire private security firms to keep their cash secure.

Use cash only when necessary. Encourage payment by check, make frequent bank deposits of cash, and write checks for payments your committee must make for services and supplies. Checks are preferable to cash because they provide a record of your payments. When cash does accumulate, get it to a safe place as soon as possible. Most banks have night depositories where you can make deposits. And school offices usually have safes where the principal can store your cash for safekeeping. It's best to avoid having individuals take cash home, even for short periods.

SAVING MONEY AND SPENDING WISELY

Most committees and individuals want to keep the costs of events within reasonable limits, so various economies must be practiced and financial decisions must be wisely made. There are a number of tried and true ways for planners to save money.

Comparison shopping can result in significant savings. "It's a mistake to order from the same catalogue or buy from the same supplier year after year without checking to see that you're getting the best prices and service that you can," cautions a school business manager who helps student leaders with financial planning. "Of course you have to consider quality and service as well as the price. The idea is to get the best value for the money spent."

Negotiating can also save you money. "We were arranging for dinners at our prom, which was being held in a large hotel," recalls one food chair. "The prices seemed high to me, so I asked if we could just have sandwiches or salad. The hotel banquet manager came up with a special menu of lower-priced items."

Some things aren't negotiable, but vendors and sales representatives frequently have a great deal of latitude in pricing and sometimes they're willing to wheel and deal in order to clinch the sale. It doesn't hurt to ask, as long as you're polite and businesslike.

Renting, rather than buying, can make sense when you need to obtain items that you're unlikely to use again or can't store easily until the next time they're needed. It's possible to rent tools, clothing, props, costumes, backdrops, tables, chairs, food service items, vehicles, booths, musical instruments, stages, bleachers, and a surprising variety of other things you might need to put on a school program. Look in the yellow pages under "Rentals." Check with party rental firms, theatrical supply houses, tuxedo and clothing rental shops, costume suppliers, and even retail firms.

Borrowing is another way to obtain needed equipment. Restaurants will sometimes lend equipment to organizers of food sales, banquets, and proms. Some funeral homes, churches, and clubs will lend chairs. If an organization or business owns what you need to use, ask if it might be available for loan. Just remember that borrowing involves responsibility to return things promptly and in good condition. Don't borrow anything that you can't afford to replace. And be sure to follow up by making absolutely sure that borrowed items are promptly returned and thank-you notes, even for small items, are written and sent as soon as possible. This follow-up is an important responsibility. Make sure that someone reliable is appointed to see that these vital tasks are carried out.

Insurance can be a good way to limit your financial risk and save money by allowing you to rent, borrow, or use facilities at lower rates. It's possible to obtain a form of insurance, called a bond, for people who will be handling funds and large amounts of cash. Sometimes you can negotiate a lower rental rate if you can prove good insurance coverage. And insurance can be a hedge against such unforeseen disasters as theft, bad weather, accidents, and lawsuits. Talk to your school's business manager or financial adviser about insurance coverage and how to obtain it at a reasonable cost.

Recycling equipment, supplies, and props may also result in significant savings. You can recycle by saving such things as props, punch bowls, crowns for the king and queen, wall hangings, and plastic streamers for use again. Keep an accurate inventory of the things designated for re-use, and be sure to store them where the next user can locate them.

Another method of recycling is to sell equipment to other groups after you have used it or purchase such things jointly with other organizations who will need it at different times than you do. "We saved more than two thousand dollars on decorations," reports a pleased prom committee chair from New Mexico. "I called the hotel where we were holding our prom on Friday night and asked if another school was booked there for Saturday. The banquet manager gave me the name of the chair of the other school's prom committee and we got together to buy some of the decorations, which were used on both nights. We were able to coordinate our themes and colors enough to share in some of the major expenses, but we each supplied enough of our own things to give each prom a distinct look and mood."

Buying used supplies and equipment is recycling, too. And sometimes you can manage to have what you need donated just by spreading the word that you're looking for specific items.

And, of course, be open to innovative ways of recycling. "We even saved money by recycling our garbage at cleanup time," says one student. "We sorted trash and used far fewer plastic trash bags than had been used the year before. It was a small savings, but every little bit helps."

4

FOOD AND REFRESHMENTS

Many school functions involve food—everything from light snacks to full-course meals. Sometimes meals are an essential part of the function, such as at an awards banquet, a baccalaureate breakfast, or a club dinner.

Going out to a good restaurant for an elegant dinner before a prom is a tradition in many communities. In other schools, a dinner or elaborate snack buffet is served at the prom itself. Fund-raising often involves the selling of snacks or food items.

Whenever food is part of an event, careful planning is necessary. If your group is fixing and selling food, for example, you may need to comply with health laws and regulations. Check with your city, county, or state health department to find out whether you need to obtain any permits or follow particular rules. Another good source of information is the food service manager or cafeteria director at your school.

FOOD SERVICE OPTIONS

When you're planning a meal, you will consider a number of different food options, depending on the location, budget, and purpose. You can have everyone who attends bring food, either to share in pot-luck style or in their own individual-meal, brown-bag style. You can prepare and serve the food yourself, arrange for a group of volunteers to prepare and serve it for your group, or hire a professional to prepare and serve the food. Caterers can bring everything with them or do the preparation at your site. Or you can book your event at a restaurant, hall, or hotel that provides complete meal service.

Parties and events that don't involve meals usually do involve snacks and beverages, so make sure that your planning for any event takes into account the appetites of those who attend. It's easy and elegant to serve a zesty punch, special cake, and snack buffet at a dance or to provide refreshments at the intermission of a school play or concert. Such treats are usually appreciated by the audience and can often be sold to help defray costs. Remember, though, that hotels and restaurants won't usually let you bring your own food or drinks. Charges for such items as punch can mount quickly. Make sure you understand how such charges will be computed before you make final arrangements.

These methods and almost endless variations and combinations of them mean that you have lots of possibilities for great meal events.

Pot Luck. An old-fashioned pot-luck meal can be elegant and delicious, suitable for even a formal banquet. The menu can be planned ahead of time and each person can be asked to bring particular items or ingredients. The resulting smorgasbord can be served buffet-style, family style at individual tables, or dished onto plates and individually served.

"If your group is operating with a tight budget, pot-luck meals are the best way I know to serve great food and keep the cost low," says one student.

48

"Be sure to plan carefully to keep service smooth if you're planning a large pot-luck dinner," warns a faculty adviser. "We put on a really elegant buffet for our prom. But we had only one long serving table and the process simply took too long. Some kids were still waiting to eat when others were finished. We should have divided the food up onto five or six serving tables, at least. We'll know better next year."

"Our craft club holds a monthly salad-bar fund raiser," says a student from a school in Mississippi. "We set up a salad bar in the school cafeteria at lunch time and charge students to fix a delicious salad plate. Everyone brings different ingredients and dressings. It's easy to organize and the proceeds help us buy craft supplies and equipment."

Catered Food Service. If you hold a meal event outdoors or at a site other than a restaurant or hotel, it's not necessary for a committee to plan the actual food preparation if you hire a caterer. Caterers can provide a range of foods and services from light snacks to full-course meals.

"Using a caterer makes a lot of sense if you want to have an elegant meal at a school event," says a Virginia teacher. "When we moved our prom back to the gym, we decided to serve a catered dinner. It was just as easy to deal with the caterer as it was to deal with the hotel where we had held previous proms. And the caterer was willing to work with us to build a menu around our prom theme."

Find professional caterers by asking around, looking in the yellow pages and newspaper advertising sections, and checking with food service experts at your own school, such as the cafeteria manager or a home economics teacher.

Sometimes you can arrange to have volunteer catering services provided by another school organization

*Then and now: Food and refreshments
are often an important part of school events.*
Above: *In this photo taken during the turn of
the century, students enjoy a formal afternoon tea.*
Below: *In a more contemporary affair, students
help themselves to a catered buffet.*

or exchange such services. In one Wisconsin high school, various school clubs provide food and service for other clubs' special dinners and parties. Each group has a specialty, such as food preparation or table service. When one organization holds a banquet, it can call on the others to put it on for them. The principal keeps track of each club's service credits and amounts of service used. "It's a great system," she says.

Parents, adult service clubs, and community groups can sometimes be called upon for catering services, either on a volunteer basis as or as a fund-raising project for their own organization. There are lots of innovative ways that groups can cooperate for their mutual benefit.

RENTING EQUIPMENT

Groups who plan formal meals at school or community sites often rent tables, tablecloths, china, silver, and serving accessories from party-rental firms. "Don't overlook rental companies when you're planning a big event," advises a Seattle party consultant. "They can provide everything you need to transform your school cafeteria or gym into an elegant banquet hall. The cost is surprisingly reasonable, too." You can rent punch fountains, platters, coffee urns, warming trays, centerpieces, and just about anything else you might need to enhance your refreshment or dinner table.

"We wanted to have our honor banquet at school, but the cafeteria tables have bench seats that just weren't right for the type of dinner we wanted," says the honor society president at an East Coast school. "Then we found out you can rent anything you need. We got tables, chairs, goblets, linen tablecloths, and napkins. We used the cafeteria plates and other supplies from the school."

RESTAURANTS AND HOTELS

Meal events can also be held at restaurants, hotels, and banquet halls, but they still require planning. Typically, the banquet manager will meet with your committee to select a menu and set a price. Your group will probably be asked to sign a contract that spells out charges and conditions. You'll pay a nonrefundable deposit. You'll probably have to provide the restaurant with an accurate count a few days ahead of time and guarantee to pay for a specific number of meals. Make sure you understand all the charges. Most banquet facilities add taxes, tips or gratuities, and other service charges to the final bill. You'll have to plan for such extra expenses. Rely on an adult adviser to guide you through the process of dealing with restaurants and hotels. This is important, since usually only an authorized adult can sign the contract.

FUND-RAISING WITH FOOD

Selling food is a popular way to raise money. Your operation can be as simple as cooling a few cans of pop in a washtub to vend from a booth at a local fair to putting on full-course dinners that people pay to attend. The simplest food sales involve buying and reselling prepackaged products such as cans of pop, candy bars, cookies, frozen pizza, fruitcakes, nuts, and snack items.

Bake sales are a perennial favorite, as are other types of pot-luck snack booths, where members of the group bring in homemade goods for resale. A variation of this is the popular and successful "Dime-a-Dip" dinners put on by a southern school. Everyone who attends must bring a salad, main dish, bread, or dessert enough to serve at least eight people as the price of admission. Then each person who eats is charged a dime for every spoonful or small serving. Big eaters, of course, pay more. Everyone has a good meal, lots of fun, and the monthly dinners raise needed funds for the school library.

School groups have success with pancake suppers, fish fries, spaghetti dinners, strawberry festivals, and ice-cream socials. "If you're going to try to put on a complete meal, it's best to get some adult help," says one school food-service manager. "Student groups usually do better preparing, serving, and selling one or two specialty items, rather than full-course meals. It makes more sense to learn by putting on a dessert buffet, for example, rather than a full dinner."

SAFETY AND SANITATION

When you're planning a picnic, banquet, pot-luck dinner, or the refreshments for a party, make sure that proper safety and sanitary precautions are taken. Cleanliness is essential, so be sure that everyone who handles food washes their hands frequently. Use only clean serving dishes and utensils. Scrub work surfaces immediately after use. Cover food to keep flies and contaminants off.

Temperature is another vital factor in the safe storage and serving of food. Salads, vegetables, and meats should be chilled or kept hot enough to inhibit the reproduction of bacteria. Set foods out at the last minute and put them away right after serving. Make sure that poultry and pork are thoroughly cooked. At picnics and outdoor events, chill foods with ice. Food will stay cooler and safer if you don't pack ice chests too full and if you don't open them too often. (The idea is to keep food either hot or cold, but not warm, since bacterial growth is inhibited by hot and cold temperatures, while bacteria thrive and reproduce in warm temperature.)

Stick to menu choices that make sense from a

safety point of view. If you can't keep food refrigerated easily, avoid eggs, mayonnaise, stuffings, and meats that spoil easily. It's safest to rely on prepackaged items and foods that keep well.

If you have any doubts about the safety of your food-handling procedures, call upon the expertise of your health department; Cooperative Extension Service; school cafeteria manager; or a friendly restaurant owner, home economics teacher, or knowledgeable parents. When working with food, you'll appreciate and probably require adult help.

5

DYNAMITE
DECORATING

Students in a Virginia school district hired a Manhattan set decorator to help them transform the school gym into a starry night in Venice for their prom. The decorator swathed the entire gym in huge fabric backdrops and created street and building facades out of theater sets. Students built gondolas and hung thousands of stars on the drapes.

"If I hadn't walked in through the front door of the school, I never would have believed we were in the gym," said one prom-goer. "It was fantastic."

The elaborate decorations cost almost as much as renting a hotel ballroom, but the prom was held in a location required by the board of education and the students had enjoyed the opportunity to participate in the transformation.

"I hate to admit it," one junior said, "but I think I had more fun working on the decorations than I did actually attending the prom. Even cleaning up was fun."

Of all the committee jobs associated with putting on a major school event, decorating can be the most rewarding. Here is a chance to work together with a large group of kids, make new friends, learn new skills, be creative, and enjoy the satisfaction of making magic.

An elaborate, big-budget event, such as a prom, can provide interesting challenges and the opportunity to be especially creative. Decorating on such a scale requires organization and teamwork. Like other jobs involved in putting on a successful school event, the key to good decorating is planning.

GETTING STARTED

The first job of the decorating committee is to determine its purpose. Much will depend on the site. Will the decorating crew be making a complete transformation of a cafeteria, gym, or other facility or will it only supplement the elegance of a hotel or banquet hall?

Decorating will be closely related to the theme of the event as well, so the decorating committee may play a major role in deciding on a theme and then implementing it. Decorations are usually expected to evoke the theme or create a special theme-related mood.

Next, available resources need to be evaluated. What types of decorating equipment are already on hand? Is there money available to buy or rent special equipment or services? Will committee members be likely to find sources of borrowed supplies? Are there limitations on types of materials that can be used? Are there school clubs, classes, or groups that might be called upon for help? Are there plenty of willing workers who can be recruited for the decorating crew right before the big event?

MAKING PLANS

Once the resources are understood, the budget is in place, and volunteers are lined up, the planning can begin. The site of the event should be measured and scale drawings or floor plans of all areas to be decorated should be made. Sometimes there is so much decorat-

*Decorating materials can be tastefully mixed
and matched to enliven any school event.*

ing to plan that the committee divides up responsibility for specific areas such as entrances and exits, ceilings, floors, walls, refreshment areas, the stage, the photographer's area, dining tables, hallways, and peripheral rooms, such as a lounge for chaperones.

Once the areas to be decorated have been decided on and assigned, planners should select colors and a motif that harmonizes with the theme. Then this overall color scheme, theme, and motif should be incorporated into all the decorated areas. It is a good idea to make sure in advance that all the decor materials you plan to use meet with fire department regulations.

TABLES

Table decorations can include tablecloths, centerpieces, flowers, place cards, favors, candles, chair covers, napkins, and place mats. Napkins, plates, and cups can be selected with the theme and color scheme in mind. Often paper napkins, place mats, candles, and glassware can be imprinted with the theme and date. Printed menus and programs can also be placed at tables. Miniature lights can sometimes be used effectively to supplement the candlelight and enhance a romantic atmosphere.

"Each table at our prom had a centerpiece made of dried flowers in a basket with tiny white Christmas lights threaded through. The lights gave a fairylike quality to the atmosphere. It was spectacular," recalls a student from Kansas who worked on her prom.

HALLWAYS

Halls and peripheral areas can be simply decorated to complement the more elaborate decorations in the main floor area, or they can be turned into special areas where students can gather to chat or relax. Try putting up displays in halls or arranging upholstered furniture in conversation groupings. One school's prom theme was "Down Memory Lane," so a series of displays was created along a painted path on the floor called, naturally, "Memory Lane." Students walked down the memory lane to see photos, souvenirs, and mementos from earlier events all arranged in a series of exhibits. "We started with baby pictures and covered all the years right up to the present," says one of the planners. "Memory Lane was a highlight of the prom."

Decorators may want to design an attractive coat-check area in a hallway and provide decorated tables and chairs for ticket takers, security personnel, and chaperones to use during the course of the evening. Plants, furniture groupings, signs on easels, streamers, and bows can all contribute to effective hallway decor.

ENTRANCES

Simple doors can be turned into enticing entrance arches through the construction of simple arch sets. Archways can be fashioned with balloons, draperies, and streamers to create a passage through which participants can enter the magical world inside.

MAIN FLOOR AREA

The ballroom floor can be transformed with such structures as gazebos and arches, arrangements of chairs, plants, and decorative accessories. Fountains, wishing wells, conversation nooks, and theme-related structures like the gondolas at the Virginia prom can be rented, built, or imaginatively created to enhance the mood.

WALLS

Walls can be draped with fabric, covered with special paper sheeting, festooned with streamers, and deco-

Top: *Decorating floor areas can add real impact to a setting. Here, students pose with several floor arrangements designed to create a special mood.*
Bottom: *A combination of accessible props and an attractive wall display in the background transform this high school gymnasium into a nostalgic fifties setting.*

rated with painted background sets to match the theme. Huge murals can be purchased or painted to create whatever environment seems appropriate. Ornamental lattice, fencing, and false shrubbery can be used to cover wall areas and create interesting nooks and crannies. Posters, banners, netting, and miniature lights all make attractive wall decorations.

CEILING

One of the most important areas to decorate is the ceiling. Here is where you can achieve stunningly dramatic effects with relatively simple techniques. When ceilings are draped with streamers or fabric in handsome patterns, covered with balloons and festooned with lanterns, chandeliers, mirror balls, stars, tissue hangings, they can make a powerful contribution to the impact and ambiance of the decorations. Ceiling decorations should be carefully mapped out on a scale plan before they are put up so that draping patterns can be most effective and decorators will be able to estimate material needs accurately.

PROGRAM AREA

The stage or band area should be decorated in such a way as to focus attention on the performers without obscuring the visibility or hampering the movement of the band members. Plain backdrops are recommended so as not to distract attention from the performers or compete with their costumes and props.

The stage can be a raised platform or a designated area of the floor set off by backdrops, waist-high dividers, or decorative fencing. If a varied program has been planned, you might have multiple stages or performance areas. They can be uniformly decorated or planned with subtle differences to enhance the impact of the performers and emphasize variety.

SUPPLIES, PROPS, AND ACCESSORIES

Plants, balloons, props, arches, furniture, streamers, banners, lights, fountains, thrones, stages, theatrical sets, fabrics, cardboard, paint, and lavish doses of imagination can be mixed and matched in endless combinations to create mood and completely transform the site into an inviting fantasy.

Decor supplies and equipment may be rented; purchased from mail-order specialty suppliers or regular retail stores; made in school shop, art, or theater classes; or begged and borrowed. It's possible to do a dazzling job with even limited funds and it's easy to recycle many decorating supplies.

GETTING HELP

There are lots of possible sources for help and advice in planning decorations within your own school. A drama, art, shop, or theater teacher, for example, may be able to show you set-construction and painting techniques that can be easily adapted for your prom or other event. The music department can help you plan stage areas. A sewing or home economics teacher might have ideas on draping fabrics and decorating table areas. Even science teachers might have decorative plants you could borrow. And the custodial staff can usually help you plan safe ways to put up and take down decorations.

Professional help, both volunteer and paid, can come from many sources, too. Interior-decorating firms, the furniture and home-décor departments of large department stores, and theatrical production firms are all possibilities. Sometimes you can get free help from the display department of a store or the manager of a large restaurant. Whenever you visit an attractively decorated place, ask yourself what you can learn by studying the ways the decorative effect was created.

Cleverly arranged balloons, columns, and drapes turn this gymnasium into a fabulous formal fantasy for the prom.

CLEANING UP

Decorating is the ideal place to unleash creativity, enlist legions of volunteers, and have a wonderful time in the process. Be sure, though, to plan for cleanup as part of the decorating process. Your school's basketball team won't want to play in the midst of a "Midnight Fantasy" setting and businesses won't want to hold their hotel meetings in rooms decorated for "Moments of Madness." So be sure to clean up carefully, recycle as many materials as possible, save useful supplies for the next time or another event, and make an inventory of decorating supplies stored for another group to use.

SAYING THANK-YOU

Don't forget to return borrowed items promptly and write thank-you notes to everyone who has contributed their advice, information, supplies, equipment, and generosity to make your school event a memorable success.

6

PROMOTION AND PUBLICITY

Good publicity attracts people to your school event and can play a big factor in making it a success. When effectively carried out, publicity rewards the efforts of committee members and volunteers with recognition. It helps recruit new committee members and workers. It increases community awareness, improves your school's image, and generates goodwill. It motivates financial contributions, brings in business, increases community support, and attracts attention to fund-raising efforts. Publicity is a key ingredient in the success of any program.

Unfortunately, the role of the publicity chair is often overlooked and misunderstood. It's a job that's too often assigned as an afterthought to filling the "important" slots. And all too often the person who has been put in charge of publicity has little idea of how to approach the job.

"I got stuck with the publicity for our senior play," says Susan, a student from Colorado. "I was new in school and I thought working on the play would help me make friends. The only slot available was publicity, so I took it, but I was terrified. I wasn't all that good in

English and I figured I'd have to do a lot of creative writing."

Susan muddled through. She made lots of posters. She got a fellow student who loved to write poetry to help her write a long, "creative" press release and sent it to the local paper. Although she was disappointed that the paper ran only a brief announcement in its regular calendar listings, the play, always a popular school event, was well attended by students, faculty, and parents. It was a success and Susan enjoyed working on it. She was drafted to help out with the stage crew on the nights of performance and attended a party for the cast and crew.

"I felt like I had contributed something, but to be honest I enjoyed the stage work much more than the publicity. I never really had a good idea of exactly what to do. It was an uncomfortable assignment."

One of the reasons that the publicity assignment was uncomfortable for Susan is that not many students or teachers really understand how to develop an organized, professional approach to publicity.

PURPOSE AND PLANNING

There's nothing magical about good publicity, although the results can seem magical. It's not necessary for the person handling publicity to be "creative," gifted in English, or talented in art. The key to effective publicity is purpose and planning.

The place to start is at the end, by identifying the results you would like your publicity to achieve. If you know the purpose of your publicity, you can plan an effective publicity program that makes the best possible use of the available tools and the talents of others to whom duties can be delegated.

As your purpose varies, so will your plan. If you are planning a fund-raising carnival, for example, one publicity goal will be to attract as many paying customers as possible. You'll also want to motivate these customers to spend as much as possible and possibly attract sponsors to make additional cash contributions. Perhaps you'll be raising funds for a specific purpose and you have an additional goal of raising public awareness of a particular community problem that you're trying to solve. Thus, your goals for this carnival are to attract customers, motivate generosity, and educate the community.

You'll have a different publicity purpose for your senior prom. Since attendance at proms is limited to class members and guests, you won't be trying to attract the general public. Your purpose will be narrower, limited to trying to get as many class members as possible to participate. You may need more committee members and helpers. If in past proms there have been problems of drinking, vandalism, or negligent student behavior, you'll want to improve the image of your school by communicating to the public what steps are being taken to reduce such problems. You'll probably want to recognize the efforts of the committee members in newspaper articles and you might want to publicize the names of the king and queen, class and club officers, and others who might be honored in the grand march. If dedicated teachers help with planning and supervision, you'll want to reward them with recognition, too.

Once you have a clear idea of the purpose of your publicity, you can make a plan. Start by establishing a timetable. Let's say that you've been made the publicity chair of your class play. You've identified the following publicity purposes:

• Attract audiences as large as possible, both from the school and the community at large.
• Find good cast members, crew members, adult advisers, wardrobe and makeup people, and committee members.

• Motivate advertisers and patrons to contribute financially to the program.
• Generate community goodwill for your school.
• Find donors of furniture and other props.
• Reward all the people who work on the production with public recognition.

Now you have somewhere to begin and a clear idea of where you want to go. Next, ask yourself what needs to be done first. In this case, recruiting is a logical place to start. As soon as the planning for the play begins, the publicity chair should be spreading the word that help is needed.

Recognition for the hard work of committee, cast, and crew members can be an ongoing process. Announce the names of participants as they are appointed or selected. This recognition will reward the workers and help attract new recruits. It will also contribute to the overall image of your school and begin to generate interest in the play itself.

Next, take a look at how you will attract people to the play and begin to think of promotional activities that will generate the necessary interest. Work hard to keep a continuing and growing public awareness that will peak just before the first performance.

Once things are well under way, investigate ways to enlist the financial support of advertisers and patrons. Plan how you will continue your publicity efforts to keep awareness and motivation high. And think about what you will need to do to wrap things up after the play.

PUBLICITY TOOLS

Once you know what you want to accomplish with your publicity and when you want to accomplish it, identify the various promotional tools you or others will use to get the job done. Publicity tools include direct communication, press releases, posters, banners, school announcements, radio and television public service announcements, flyers and brochures, articles and photos in school publications, promotional activities, preview mini-programs, buttons, and programs.

To recruit volunteers from within the school, you'll want to use school announcements, posters, the school newspaper, and direct contact. You'll publicize organizational meetings and appeal for volunteers to fill specific slots. If you want to solicit help from the wider community, you'll expand your efforts to include direct contact with businesses and individuals who might help and perhaps print a general appeal in a local newspaper. You'll adjust your methods and fine-tune your publicity program as your purpose is met and the various slots are filled. You might start out with a flurry of publicity for an organizational meeting, urging anyone with an interest to attend. Later, if you have most slots filled but the committee still needs ushers, for example, or a refreshment chair, you can put up posters that list these specific vacancies and arrange for short announcements. Once recruitment is completed, your focus will shift to your other publicity goals.

If you want to attract paying customers from the community, you'll use posters, banners, public-service announcements, special promotions, and short press releases to interest people and motivate them to come. Since most people prefer to assimilate information in short, manageable bites and since repetition is a key to success, you'll want to keep press releases short, focused, and frequent.

Another highly successful publicity technique is the special event. Maybe you can put on a short scene or preview of your show at a local mall. Perhaps you can schedule a television appearance for cast members. You might have costumed cast members walk through the business district of your community, passing out flyers or handbills. You can use tickets to your event for prizes on radio shows or at other fund-raising events in exchange for publicity. Here's a chance to give your creativity full reign.

After you've developed a publicity plan that identifies publicity purposes and designates the best tools and techniques to meet the goals, you'll need to find and cultivate the right people to get the jobs done. It's not necessary for the publicity chair to be a great writer if she can find someone to produce press releases on a specific schedule. And the person in charge of publicity doesn't need any artistic skill if he or she looks for talented artists to whom to delegate the responsibility for painting posters and banners. A shy publicity coordinator can usually find others to solicit support of local businesses.

The idea isn't to find all the requisite skills in a single person. Instead, an effective publicity chair will decide on a purpose, devise an overall publicity plan, identify specific tasks, and then find people to do each job. Most volunteers are grateful to be assigned a concrete task. It's easy to ask someone to design and draw six posters or to work with a crew that will paint a single banner. You're sure to find someone willing to write and submit a series of five specific press releases. If you can identify specific tasks and tools, then delegate jobs, you'll have a successful publicity program.

Once the planning is under way, the publicity chair will turn to specific tools to get the job done.

Press releases are the traditional backbone of publicity. A press release is a brief news story or a fact sheet from which a news story can be prepared that is sent to newspapers. Good press releases should be brief, clear, targeted, and tightly focused. There's a popular misconception that press releases should be "creative," clever, long, and detailed. Actually, the opposite is true.

If you have a great deal of information to impart, think in terms of a series of press releases, each with a specific purpose and a clear focus, rather than a single, long one. Write it in the inverted pyramid style, with the essential information—the who, where, what, when, and why—distilled in the very first paragraph. Lead with the most interesting or most important fact. Be as concise as possible. Then continue with other information in declining order of importance. The reason for this style is so that a press release can be cut from the bottom up according to the space limitations of the paper. The story should make complete sense, even if it is cut to a single paragraph.

Each press release should have a tight focus. One might announce the setting of a date for an event. Another could focus on the selection of a chair and key leaders. The next could announce the theme of an event. Don't try to cover more than one subject in a release. See page 71 for a sample press release.

Each press release should be carefully targeted. What type of newspaper are you sending it to? What is entirely appropriate for your community weekly newspaper might not be right for a regional daily. Study the other news in the newspapers you plan to send press releases to. If the regional daily doesn't ever cover homecomings, school plays, and proms, it won't cover yours, either, even if you send a masterful press release. If it does give coverage to such events, make sure your press release follows a similar format. Your community weekly paper will be far more receptive to school coverage and you'll have more flexibility. This will be a main source of publicity, so study the paper carefully and send it a series of well-planned press releases.

There's a difference between your community weekly paper and an all-advertising publication. Don't pay to advertise in the latter publication and then expect your weekly newspaper to print your press releases. If you do pay for any advertising, divide your advertising budget fairly between publications.

If your school publishes a newspaper, be sure to contact the editor early in order to arrange for maxi-

SAMPLE PRESS RELEASE

TO: Centerville Journal
14 West Main Street
Centerville, NY 14140

FOR: Immediate Release

FROM: Stella Brendon, Publicity Chair
Centerville High School Prom Committee
555-7721, school; 555-3155, home

CENTERVILLE PROM COMMITTEE NAMES
STUDENT LEADERS

Julie Stewart, a member of the senior class at Centerville High School has been named chair of "Horizons Unlimited," the 1991 Senior Class Prom to be held June 17 in the high school gym. Other members of the prom steering committee include: Jason Richards, co-chair; Kathy Janczyk, decorations; Martha Kopinski, finance; Bryce Carson, food; Marcia Thomas, program; Stella Brendon, publicity; and Jake Battaglia, arrangements. Mrs. Susan Farraday, an English teacher and senior class adviser, is faculty adviser to the prom committee.

"For the past several years, the senior prom has been held at a Buffalo hotel, but this year, after conducting a survey of the class, we decided to hold the prom right at the school," Stewart says. "There are several reasons for the change back to the gym. First, the principal and the board of education have encouraged our class to make the prom safer and keep costs down so that more members of the class could afford to attend. And second, we think the challenge of decorating the gym and handling more of the details ourselves will offer us a more meaningful experience."

The committee is now looking for volunteers to help with the planning. "Any students who want to serve on one of our committees should contact me or the appropriate committee chair," Stewart says. "We also need parents to help and local businesses to donate supplies, prizes and money." Adult volunteers or contributers should call the school at 555-7721.

mum publicity. And don't overlook the continuing value of yearbook coverage for annual events. Contact the yearbook editor and ask how you can help by providing information and photos.

Public-service announcements are brief commercials for radio and television that stations often run free as a community service. Most public-service announcements should be no longer than the first two sentences of a press release, condensing the essential facts into an announcement that takes only a few seconds to read out loud. Once your announcement is written, read it out loud several times and have someone listen to see if it gets the point across effectively. Keep track of the time it takes to read the announcement at a moderate pace and write the number of seconds at the top. Ten seconds is about right. It's not essential to time your public-service announcements, but it can help and it's not likely to hurt.

Sometimes it is possible to arrange for news coverage of an event. Send a fact sheet with the essential information to the attention of the news director at the station. If you would like to try to arrange for appearances on local talk shows, call the station and ask for the name of the appropriate person to talk with.

Always type press releases, fact sheets, cover letters, and public-service announcements. Be sure to use a high-quality printer, double space the copy, and include the name and telephone number of a contact person. Proofread your release for accuracy and pay special attention to the spellings of names. The publicity chair should verify the correct spelling of all names and keep an accurate list. There is no surer way to offend people than to misspell their names.

Posters, signs, handbills, and banners are another major way to publicize your event. You can't have too many, so urge everyone who has anything to do with the event to contribute one or more hand-painted posters. You might arrange to have the best duplicated for mass distribution. Make sure each one contains all the essential facts. Examples of prom posters are provided on page 74.

Posters can easily be distributed throughout the school and community. Make sure you have permission to put them up and that you observe any rules. Be sure to follow up after the event and take down any posters or signs.

Special events are a great way to generate publicity. Ask yourself what you can plan to create interest at places where people gather: a concert, talent show, or play? Develop a preview scene or mini-performance that you can take on the road to area malls, flea markets, and festivals.

Have people dressed in costume circulate through crowds to distribute handbills. Set up a booth at a fair, mall, flea market, supermarket, or other high-traffic location to distribute information.

Look for cross-event publicity opportunities. Your prom committee, for example, could decorate a float for the homecoming parade in order to generate early student and community interest. Perhaps you can trade program-advertising space with other school-event planners or work together on joint promotional events.

Buttons, T-shirts, banners, and other promotional items can turn your classmates into walking billboards. Sale of such items can help raise funds, too. Promotional merchandise can range from one-of-a-kind, hand-made items to printed bumper stickers, buttons, or T-shirts. Brain-storm for fresh ideas on how to create promotional clothes and objects. Have a T-shirt painting contest. Stencil inexpensive painters' hats. Look for area merchants who might be willing to donate promotional merchandise. The possibilities are limitless.

Programs, tickets, and other printed materials also serve a limited publicity function, although responsibility for them is often delegated to other committees. The publicity chair should look for effective ways to

JUNIORS AND SENIORS;

COME TO THE TROPICAL SERENADE

ANNUAL JUNIOR/SENIOR PROM
SATURDAY, MAY 12
8PM TO 2AM
HYATT HOTEL
$25 PER COUPLE
INCLUDES DINNER

TICKETS MUST BE PURCHASED IN _ADVANCE_

LAST DAY TO BUY TICKETS IS
THURSDAY, MAY 10

TICKETS AVAILABLE IN THE:
MAIN OFFICE,
GUIDANCE OFFICE, AND
ATHLETIC OFFICE

ATTENTION, JUNIORS!

MEETING
TUESDAY
AFTERNOON
3:00 PM
ROOM 102

YOUR PROM COMMITTEE NEEDS YOU!

HELP WITH PLANNING, DECORATIONS,
REFRESHMENTS AND, "UGH", CLEANUP!

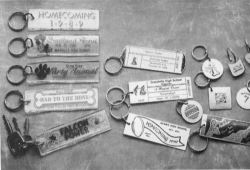

A number of catalogue companies supply party and prom items.
Posters and handbills, and printed buttons and glasses can
serve as publicity tools. These souvenir key chains
(bottom right) *can double as tickets and safety reminders.*

cooperate with students who are arranging for programs and tickets.

Remember that successful publicity is the result of purpose—knowing exactly what you want the various elements of your publicity campaign to accomplish. Once a purpose is established, careful planning can help meet your publicity goals.

7

PUTTING ON A PROM

A prom is a traditional, formal class dance that many regard as an important threshold for young people, from teenager to adult. The high school prom is often a teen's first truly adult social event. The word "prom" is probably derived from the term "promenade," the opening procession of a formal society dance. School proms evolved from the custom of socially prominent young women being presented to society at a formal debut, often a ball. Over the years the debutante tradition has ebbed, but proms have grown into annual rites of passage for high school students from all backgrounds.

PROMS OF YESTERYEAR

Although proms are well entrenched today, they are a relatively new school custom, going back only a few decades. Most schools didn't hold dances at all in the early part of this century. Social functions at many schools were limited to such gentle events as teas. In the twenties and thirties a few schools began to stage afternoon dancing functions. These tea dances, along with the debutante balls of the wealthy, were the predecessors of the prom.

By the forties and fifties dances had moved to the evening. In the forties the term prom came into common usage. It meant a dressy dance, one intended to be a big occasion. Proms were almost always held at the school. They were usually given by alumni or community adults and costs were kept modest. Girls wore party dresses and boys wore suits and ties.

During the fifties and sixties, proms grew more formal, more expensive, and more elaborate. More and more they were held away from the school in a more elegant setting. Hotels, country clubs, and convention centers became more common sites than the school gym. At the same time, students rather than adults put on proms, either for their own class or sometimes as hosts for the class before or behind them.

During the seventies and eighties, proms grew in scope, and began to rival weddings as pinnacle social events. Dresses became more daring and more expensive. Prom night expanded to include a lavish dinner in an elegant restaurant beforehand and a round of parties afterward. In some schools, students competed to spend the most and outdo each other with extravagant fashions, food, and transportation.

As prom night grew more formal and more lavish, it also became controversial. An unfortunate feature of many pre- and postprom parties during the seventies and eighties was heavy drinking that frequently led to serious accidents. Fatal automobile accidents involving drunken teens became almost an annual ritual in some communities. Fights broke out at some proms. Heavy drinking and drug use were alarmingly frequent. Peer pressure built to a peak and many students found themselves indulging in sexual relations, heavy spending, and reckless behavior, along with drinking and drug use. A few proms were cancelled as the expense and controversy mounted.

*Embarking on an evening of magic:
In 1954, a young couple gets all dressed up
for the annual prom.*

Left: *This prom, celebrated during the 1940s, was held in the afternoon in the school gymnasium. This 1990s prom (below) was also staged in the school gym, but was an evening affair. Dress attire has become more formal at modern proms.*

In the nineties, though, proms seem to be safer, better organized, and more interesting than ever before. "The pendulum seems to be swinging back," notes one teacher. "The kids are having a good time, but they're working with parents and teachers to make their proms safe, fun, and affordable."

There seems to be a trend back to the school gym, or to nontraditional and interesting facilities. Plenty of proms are still held in hotels and elegant ballrooms, though. Students are getting more heavily involved in the planning and more parents are getting into the act than ever before. Post-prom parties are being made into an official part of the festivities and many all-night bashes are planned by parents and community leaders to keep the evening safe. Prizes, entertainment, and an interesting array of activities are offered as incentives to keep the students in safe surroundings and out of trouble.

"The prom is the ultimate school dance, the pinnacle of school social events," observes a teacher from Minnesota. "It can be the best evening of your life or a bitter disappointment. It all depends on how well you plan."

PLANNING THE PROM

The skills needed to put on a prom are the same ones vital to putting on other school programs. If you know how to plan a prom, you'll be able to use the same techniques to plan more modest programs, such as class dances and awards ceremonies. You'll also be able to plan events of even greater scope, such as homecoming pageants, fund-raising fairs, or major festivals.

The following guidelines should help pave the way to a successful high school prom:

Setting Up Committees. Every school is different and each planning situation is unique, but certain committees will probably be useful. The central or major committee will probably include a mix of interested students, class officers, adult advisers, and school administrators. Parents might be involved, too.

Most proms are put on by the junior or senior class and coordinated by the class adviser. In your school, the committee structure may be already in place, making it easier to get started. If you have ideas for changing the structure, it's fine to speak up early in the planning process. It's a good idea, though, to tamper only lightly with a functioning system. There's an old adage, "If it ain't broke, don't fix it"—sound advice for planners. Start with a modest planning committee, choose a student chair, and clarify the role of the class adviser. Then set up other committees as specific needs and responsibilities are identified.

Setting the Date. The traditional prom season is May and June, but other dates during the school year are sometimes used. It is vital to decide on a date early. A year and a half in advance is not too soon. The date will depend on several things, including the dates of other school and community events, the availability of facilities, local traditions, and such factors as climate. If your prom is traditionally held in the school gym, for example, you might have more flexibility in setting the date than if you have to book an outside facility where proms from other schools might be scheduled. If you live in a warm climate, you may have to schedule your prom for earlier in the spring or limit yourself to an air-conditioned facility.

Selecting the Place. Deciding on a location is another thing that must be done as early as possible. It used to be that almost all proms were held in the school gym. In the last few decades, many schools have used more elegant locations such as hotel ballrooms or convention centers, but today there seems to be a move back to the gym in some communities. Surprisingly, many students seem to prefer having their proms at the school.

81

"We had a great time when we were putting up the decorations," says Brian from Texas. "Even the cleanup wasn't bad. I really felt like I had a stake in things. I was proud to escort my date to our "Midsummer Night's Dream." The gym looked sensational and she seemed impressed with what we had accomplished. Inside, you couldn't even tell it was a school."

"Our gym isn't big enough," says a North Carolina teacher who advises the junior class. "In my school two classes attend each prom because the juniors put on the prom for the seniors. Lots of kids bring dates from other schools and we have a large school, so we have to plan on having attendance of a thousand to twelve hundred. We usually go to one of the large hotels. One year we used the convention center."

Weather can be a factor, too. A class in rural New York State held its prom on board an excursion boat. "We wanted to do something different," says a member of the prom committee. "We're a small school, so we could all fit on the boat. The night was cold and rainy, though. People had a good time anyway, but we probably won't try it again."

A West Coast senior class held its prom in the marble lobby of a large bank. A restored mansion used as a community center and museum served as the setting for a New England prom. In a Midwestern city, students danced in the courtyard of the local art gallery. Railroad stations, convention centers, corporate headquarters buildings, museums, boats, clubs and guard halls at military bases, shopping malls, department stores, and even factories have all been settings for imaginative proms.

Your choice of a site may have already been determined by factors outside of student control. If the school board has already decided that the prom must be held at the school, you'll either have to go along with the board's decision or appeal it if you have strong feelings about where you want to hold your prom.

If you're having a prom somewhere away from school, students and an adult adviser will have to "shop" for potential sites and make arrangements. You'll need adult help for this stage in planning, since many hotels, restaurants, and convention centers will not deal with students alone. Booking a hotel facility or banquet hall usually involves signing a contract, which is something students cannot usually do. In many schools, the principal is the only one who can approve and sign such a contract. Check with your faculty adviser to find out what your school requires.

When deciding where to hold the prom, consider the wishes of students, the expected attendance and the capacity of the facility, the rules and requirements of your school, the available funds, and the amount of help you can expect in decorating and planning the event.

Setting Up a Budget. An important committee function will be to decide how much you can afford to spend on your prom, where that money will come from, how much is already on hand and how much, if anything, students will be charged for tickets. Once you know how much money is available, other decisions can be made. This often means compromise and adjustment in order to have an elegant and affordable prom. Money management is covered in detail in Chapter Three.

Choosing a Theme. The theme is what makes your prom really special and most committees put a lot of effort and discussion into deciding on the theme. Some themes are based on romance, some on friendship. Some have geographic implications. "An Evening in Venice," "Lights of London," or "Moonlight Bay" are examples. Themes can be based on a season, a special song, a favorite piece of literature, or the passage of time. The only limitation on finding a special theme that's exactly right for your class is the imaginations of the planners. Try to keep your theme specific enough to be meaningful and evocative, yet broad enough to tie in easily with school or class traditions, the decorations, menu, entertainment, and music. This can be an enjoyable and creative process. See page 85 for a list of suggested themes.

Refreshments. Prom night will certainly involve refreshments during the evening, and often one or more full-course meals. Your committee will have to decide if you want to incorporate such meals as a dinner, midnight buffet, or postprom breakfast. And you'll have to plan for drinks and light snacks throughout the evening. Again, if you use the services of a restaurant, caterer, hotel, or convention center, you'll need an adult to accompany you and you'll need to have an appropriate adult sign any resulting contracts. Chapter Four includes more details about food and refreshments.

Decorations. Decorating for your prom will be a major activity. The decorating committee, or committees, will be working to translate the theme into a magical reality. Specific suggestions are included in Chapter Five.

Music. Another decision your committee will have to make is what kind of music to have. Some schools prefer live bands while others opt for recorded sound systems, which are growing in popularity because of the often-lower expense and the high sound quality it is possible to achieve. Many schools use more than one type of music and perhaps even more than one live band. At some proms, the professional band is spelled at breaks by student musicians and disk jockeys.

Planners should start thinking about music as soon as the date is set. Select a band and/or sound system as early as possible. Be sure you get an opportunity to hear the band perform before booking it. In some communities, booking agents for bands schedule general auditions. And have your finance committee and faculty adviser review and obtain official approval of any contracts.

THEMES TO THINK ABOUT
FOR PROMS AND DANCES

Use this chart to get you started on the process of selecting a theme and as an inspiration for your brainstorming.

Category	Sub-Category	Themes
TIME	Seasons Night and Day Months Hours Years Minutes Moments Seconds Forever Eternity	Spring Magic — A Night to Remember — This Magic Moment — As Time Goes By — Moments of Magic — A Little Night Music — Starry Night in Centerville — Minute by Minute, Hour by Hour — Days of Wonder, Nights of Magic — Dream Days — The Night Belongs to the Young — Friends Forever — Eternal Magic — Don't Let It End — Memories of Tomorrow — We've Got Tonight — Somewhere in Time
FEELINGS, EMOTIONS	Love Romance Friendships Fantasy Loyalty Remembrance	Together Again — Love Will Keep Us Together — Thanks for the Memories — Magic Memories — We'll Always Remember — Never Forget — Good Times, Good Friends — True to Our School — Forever Yours — True to Each Other — True to Ourselves — When I'm with You — Celebration of Love — Keep Believing
GEOGRAPHY	Places Climate Regions	Hawaiian Paradise — Sunny Days, Dreamy Nights — California Sunshine — Search for a Rainbow — A Night in Paradise — Almost There — Camelot — A Night in Venice *- Reach for A STAR -*
MUSIC EVENTS COLORS MOODS		Academy Awards — Rhapsody in Blue — Our Blue Heaven — Stairway to Heaven — Endless Love — Celebrate! — Looks Like We Made It — Puttin' on the Ritz — When You Wish Upon a Star

Invitations, Favors, Tickets, Printed Programs, Souvenirs, and Memory Books. Mementos will enhance your prom. Printed programs can be elaborate and elegant or simple and inexpensive. They should list all the committees and acknowledge the contributions of prizes, cash, and time from the community. They should also list the schedule of the evening's events. Programs can also have spaces for autographs, dance cards, photos, and other special memory joggers.

SAMPLE INVITATION

The Junior Class of

Midland High School

requests the pleasure of your company

at the

Junior-Senior Prom

on Saturday, the eighteenth of May

Nineteen hundred and ninety-one

at six o'clock in the evening

High School Gymnasium

R.S.V.P.

Most schools arrange to have one or more special gifts for each couple or person attending the prom. These can include goblets, key chains, candles, garters, scrolls, plaques, and other imprinted or engraved items.

A number of companies specialize in selling such items to schools and publish catalogues to order from. A list of firms that will usually send catalogues and helpful information on request is found in the bibliography.

Committee members can also shop locally at jewelers, remembrance shops, and advertising specialty suppliers. It is often possible to rent equipment to engrave or personalize the mementos. Some souvenirs can be crafted by students or made by specialty classes. A horticulture class in New York State, for example, arranges mini-baskets of dried flowers for each place at the dinner table. The tiny baskets each have a ribbon imprinted with the theme of the prom and the date. If you enlist the help of talented artisans among your student body, an imaginative variety of hand-crafted items may be available for favors, decorations, gifts, and prizes.

Photographs. Many schools arrange to have a professional photographer set up at the prom and take pictures of all the couples, making packages of prints available at prearranged prices. If you do this, be sure to book the photographer as early as possible and interview a number of studios to find the best combination of prices, service, and quality. Some photographers, as part of their contract package, provide souvenir books with photos of each couple and a variety of candid shots from the big night. The cost of such special extras can be included in the ticket price or paid for by individual students as an option.

"If you will have a large attendance at your prom, you may need more than one photographer," says one class adviser. "When booking photographic services,

*Some students hire a professional photographer
to capture the magic of the prom.*

ask each studio how they intend to set up, what they
will charge, and how many couples they can comfortably photograph during the course of the evening.
Sometimes it's a good idea to arrange for two or three
different studios to set up and offer a variety of plans."

The photographer, or photographers, will need a
place to work. A separate room or area is best. "And
make sure to ask if the professional photographer will
allow students to take pictures of each other when the
official pictures are being taken," advises a parent who
helped make the photography arrangements at an Arkansas prom. "The photographer we contracted with
provided the lighting for a separate student area, but
wouldn't allow other photography while he was working at the main set."

"Don't forget to coordinate with the school newspaper and yearbook photography staff," says a student. "Pictures preserve memories."

Some prom committees also arrange for videotape coverage of the evening, either by a professional or by student organizations. With the proliferation of VCRs and video cameras, this can be fun, but many schools who have experimented with professional video production have decided not to do it again, since there are some disadvantages.

In order to shoot, edit, and duplicate a video of a particular event, a professional studio must charge a high price for each tape and must have a guaranteed minimum sale. Often the resulting tape is too expensive for students to buy.

"Another problem with videotape," says a teacher whose school tried video yearbooks with prom coverage included, "is that if you include every student, as you must, you end up with a tape that is long and boring. We found that sales of our video yearbook the first year were quite good, but that very few students bought a tape the second year. I think that's because they all found out that it's inconvenient to load the VCR, find the spot on the tape that shows them or interests them, rewind it and store it. It turned out to be a good idea in theory, but not a very practical one."

Some students may bring their own video cameras to the prom and you may have planned for official video coverage by a school group. If so, establish a separate, well-lighted area for videotaping and make rules about where and when taping of the evening is appropriate, since the lighting can be intrusive. You may also need to work with your security or safety committee to plan a safe place where students can leave bulky equipment while it's not in use.

The Program. Your prom can really sparkle if you develop a varied and lively program. This is an area that lends itself to creativity and can enhance the fun without adding to the cost. Surprisingly, many proms have just an evening of dancing without any organized program at all.

89

"I was astonished by the difference between the proms at my boyfriend's school and my school," reports Karen, a Nebraska senior. "We had a grand march led by all the class officers, committee members, club presidents, and other dignitaries. There was a master of ceremonies, a local radio personality, who introduced the music and special dances. At midnight we had coronation ceremonies for the king and queen. And throughout the evening there were drawings for door prizes and the presentation of various awards."

It was different at her boyfriend's school. "The band was playing when we arrived," Karen said. "It just kept going and people danced and milled around. The only announcements were when the band leader said they were taking a break. That prom wasn't nearly as much fun."

Schedule a variety of interesting and traditional events to make your prom special. When the band takes a break, have a talented school vocal group perform a number or two. Hire or enlist volunteer entertainers such as magicians, hypnotists, comics, or singers. Have them perform in between band segments or offer continuous entertainment in other rooms.

Plan specialty dances, such as a broom dance or circle dance, to get people mixing and having a good time. For a broom dance, decorate two brooms to look like a whimsical boy and girl. Pick any couple and give each person one of the brooms. Start the music and have the victims dance a few moments with their respective brooms. Stop the music and have each person present the broom to someone else. After they've given away the broom, have them invite a different partner to dance until the next switch.

For a circle dance, couples form two circles around the edge of the dance floor, boys on the outside and girls on the inside. The music starts and the circles move in opposite directions. When it stops, everyone dances with the person opposite them. Crown a king and queen and hold a coronation dance where the king and queen dance together for a few moments, then the music stops and they each ask another to dance. The music keeps stopping and couples split, each finding another dancer until everyone is on the floor with a different partner.

The actual selection of the king and queen, their attendants, and others to be honored during the program should be made ahead of time, although the identities can be kept secret until the big moment. Some schools hold a simple class election to pick the king and queen. Others stage a contest or pageant. In many schools the ranking male and female class officers serve as king and queen.

An adviser in the Pacific Northwest describes one particularly good way to choose a king and queen. "Our 'royal court' included all class officers, the top ten ranking academic students, presidents of student clubs who were also class members, captains of athletic teams, and other student leaders chosen by a committee of teachers. Ahead of time, we sold 'ballots' for fifty cents each, with a limit of ten. We put pictures of each of these outstanding students over ballot boxes at the entrances as people arrived at the prom. Students could vote as they arrived for one or more candidates. The boy and girl with the most votes were named king and queen. The money raised by selling ballots was used to help keep costs of the prom down. It was fun and it was fair."

Use a rich variety of entertainment and activities to inject magic into your prom program. Hold contests, races, and games of skill. Try to weave the evening's theme throughout the activities. Be imaginative, enterprising, and innovative. Ask for help if you need it. If, for example, you don't know how to plan a grand march or specialty dance, you can usually get instructions or advice from adults in your school and community. Ask a physical education teacher, music teacher, dance instructor, or drama coach for suggestions. Your school librarian is another valuable resource in tracking down information about planning program specifics. Other sources of program ideas and leaders include local radio stations, amateur theater groups, business organizations, and parents. Spread the word that you're looking for help. You'll be surprised at the interesting program ideas that come up. Your biggest problem will be fitting all the good ideas into your evening program. Plan your schedule carefully and make good use of the timed agenda. A sample timed agenda is provided on page 93.

Supervision. Your prom will need adult supervision, of course, so you'll be inviting enough chaperones to allow a significant adult presence in activity areas, rest rooms, cloak rooms, hallways, entrances, and on the dance floor. You should also plan to invite enough chaperones so that each one has only a limited period of "duty." Chaperones can be teachers, administrators, and even community leaders. It is a tradition for the mayor of one Southwestern small town to attend the high school prom each year. Be sure to provide an appropriate thank-you gift for each chaperone and follow up with a hand-written thank-you note.

It's a nice idea to have a separate room where chaperones can relax and visit when they're not "on duty." Your class adviser or principal can help you set up a reasonable schedule and keep you informed of any specific supervision requirements set by your school. Remember that chaperones are usually your guests and that the costs of their refreshments, flowers, and mementos should be fully covered.

Security and Safety. Very serious people problems arise when drug use, drinking, rowdy behavior, crime, and fights develop. These are problems that students

TIMED AGENDA FOR THE PROM

6:00–7:30	Arrival of Committee Chairs, Class Advisers, and Head Chaperone. Setup of check-in table. Check decorations and make sure everything is ready. Find hotel rep and confirm all last-minute details.
7:30–9:00	Arrival of Guests. Check in and signing of rules. Distribution of programs and memory books. Receiving line and greeting of guests.
8:30	Sound system starts with quiet background music. Serving of punch begins. Photography begins in Meeting Rooms 1 and 2.
8:30–11:30	Photography
9:00–9:20	Welcome by Emcee Brad Higgins, Grand March
9:25–10:00	General Dancing
10:00–10:20	Square Dance called by Mr. Volkert
10:25–11:00	Novelty Dances/Sound System/Brad
11:00–11:45	General Dancing
12:00–12:15	Coronation Ceremony and Royal Dance
12:15– 1:00	General Dancing, Snack Buffet
1:00	Last Dance and Goodnights. Catch buses for rides to school for all-night party sponsored by Parents United.
1:15	Prom chair and adviser meet with hotel banquet manager to review final bill and pay balance due.

*The timetable above is usually only distributed
to the chairs of key committees responsible for the
evening's event. A general program is distributed
to the participants and guests.*

should *not* try to handle. "No student should be put in the position of having to discipline another," says a principal. "That's what advisers and administrators are for."

Understanding your role and knowing its limitations will help you differentiate between situations you can handle yourself and occasions when you need to ask for help. Discipline is an adult function, pure and simple. If a group of outsiders crashes a homecoming dance, irresponsible students spike the punch with vodka, or one student notices another one stealing, the only appropriate response is to get adult help.

Sometimes, though, the student needs to be the one to recognize those limits. Contrary to popular belief, adult advisers aren't infallible and they sometimes make mistakes, too. "I was on the prom committee and one of the parents who was helping tried to assign me as a rest-room monitor," one girl said. "At first I said I'd do it, but then I got to thinking about it and I realized that the last place I wanted to be was stuck in the bathroom to fink on my friends if they decided to sneak a drink or a cigarette. I went to the parent and asked to be given a different assignment."

This student did the right thing in sticking up for herself. Such ability will serve her well in dealing with her peers, too. Many personal problems that come up at school events are the result of caving in to peer pressure. Prevention comes from developing a healthy sense of self-esteem, learning to stick up for yourself, and using peer pressure as a powerful tool by exerting it in a positive way.

Students are getting more involved in using positive peer pressure to save lives by discouraging drinking and driving. A number of innovative programs have been developed to help reduce the highway carnage. These range from designated driver plans to highly organized programs such as SADD (Students

Against Drunk Driving), which offers help in planning assembly programs and the nationally publicized "Contract for Life."

If you want help in planning programs to eliminate drinking and driving among students at your prom or other school event, you may obtain ideas, information, and inspiration from these organizations:

MADD (Mothers Against Drunk Driving)
669 Airport Freeway, Suite 310
Houston, TX 76053

PTA (Parent Teacher Association)
   Program Department
700 N. Rush Street
Chicago, IL 60611

RID (Remove Intoxicated Drivers)
P.O. Box 520
Schenectady, NY 12301

SADD (Students Against Drunk Driving)
10812 Ashfield Road
Adelphi, MD 20783

Your committee can plan other ways to encourage good behavior at the prom and at other school functions and to discourage drinking and drug-taking. Print the rules (for a sample list, see page 96) right on the backs of prom invitations and tickets and require entering students to sign an acknowledgment that they have read, understand, and agree to abide by the rules. Keychains and souvenirs can be imprinted with a "Don't Drink and Drive" message.

At many proms, students are "locked in," not allowed to return once they have decided to leave. "This cuts down on such things as sneaking out to the parking lot to polish off a six-pack," says one planner.

Students are also being offered attractive positive

PROM RULES

Read this list of rules carefully. Before you are issued
your tickets, you will be asked to acknowledge that you
understand each of these rules and agree to abide by
all of them.

1. Attendance at the Prom will be limited to members
    of the Junior and Senior Classes and their dates.
    Dates must be tenth graders or older. Written per-
    mission from the principal must be obtained to
    bring a date under age 15 or older than 21.

2. All those who attend must have a ticket that has
    been obtained and paid for ahead of time. No
    tickets will be sold at the door and no one without
    a ticket will be admitted.

3. You must arrive by 10:00 PM. After that, the doors
    will be closed and people will no longer be admit-
    ted, even if they have tickets.

4. Any student who leaves the dance (even to go out
    to a car) will be barred from coming back in.

5. No one will be admitted who has been drinking or
    using drugs, who smells of alcohol, or who, in the
    opinion of the head chaperone, appears inebriated.
    Anyone caught drinking, using drugs, or engaging
    in unacceptable behavior will be required to leave.
    Parents or police will be called to get inebriated
    students safely home. Such students may face fur-
    ther legal or disciplinary action.

6. All those attending will be expected to behave in a
    manner that reflects positively on our school and
    enhances the enjoyment of everyone.

reinforcement in the form of supervised post-prom parties that use a combination of entertainment, activities, and lavish prizes to entice partiers to stay in, have fun, and stay sober. It's becoming a tradition in many communities for the prom festivities to last all night long.

"Our prom was held at a downtown hotel, but then we all went back to the school afterward," says one student. "Parents and teachers had organized activities all night long. There were lots of casino-type games and contests. We were 'locked in' the school and we each signed a pledge that we wouldn't drink. If we stayed all night we were eligible for some great prizes."

Usually these parties are planned by parents and teachers, but students are getting more involved as the trend continues. If such programs are not yet available at your school, ask your principal to solicit the help of parents, law-enforcement authorities, and community leaders in planning one.

An alarming trend in some places is the rental of hotel rooms by students, often with the cooperation of ignorant parents, for prom-night parties. Some highly publicized disasters, where unruly students caused extensive damage, have resulted in an increase in both the number of prom committees that discourage this activity and also the number of hotels, school districts, and parent groups who are working to eliminate such destructive happenings.

In spite of everyone's best prevention efforts, no prom will be completely drug or alcohol free, so plans have to be made to deal with students, and occasionally adults, who are inebriated or high. "I'd really prefer to think it's not going to happen, but I'd be kidding myself," says a principal. The answer is to work with adults on a security plan for your prom that meets the needs and requirements of your school. Recognize that it's adults who will have to deal with any obvious cases of drunkenness, violence, or drug use, so there should be plenty of adult supervision. Even the adults should defer to a legally responsible school official for help in handling the worst situations.

"I was glad for all the parents, teachers, and other chaperones at our prom," says one student. "It took the burden off me. I didn't have to deal with a lot of pressure from the other kids."

8

GOING TO THE PROM

Putting on a prom, of course, takes extensive planning and organizing. Even students who just want to attend and have a good time will have to do a great deal of planning. You'll need to find a date, save enough money, get your clothing and accessories, and arrange for such things as transportation, flowers, and pre- and postprom entertainment.

GETTING A DATE

In the old days, boys asked girls for a date to the prom and a girl who wasn't invited had to stay home. But times have changed and it's considered appropriate for anyone to issue a prom invitation. If there's someone you want to go with, ask. If the person declines, ask someone else. Many students attend a prom with a friend rather than a romantic interest.

Sometimes girls and boys go to the prom in a group, without individual dates. Getting a group together, with the same number of girls and boys, can be a great way of cutting costs, having fun, and avoiding the agony of finding a date.

WHAT TO WEAR

For girls, finding the right dress can be a massive undertaking. This will involve careful shopping and perhaps compromise on price and style. Boys will probably need to rent a tuxedo. These arrangements should be made several weeks ahead of time, at least. Several months would be an even better lead time.

FLOWERS AND FRILLS

At most proms, it's traditional to wear flowers and garters. Usually the boy gets a corsage for the girl and the girl obtains a frilly souvenir garter, which she wears on one leg and later gives to her date as a souvenir. Girls often get flowers to pin on their dates' lapels, too. Ask which custom is traditional at your school. In many schools, garters and souvenirs are made available by the prom-planning committee.

GETTING THERE

Transportation to and from the prom takes planning, too. Some couples will use the family car or arrange to be chauffeured to and from the prom by a parent or other adult. Hiring a limousine service is growing into a popular way to get to proms. The cost can be quite reasonable if it is divided among several couples.

A South Dakota student arranged for a group to arrive by hay wagon, with the wagon and horses both specially decorated for the occasion. The volunteer fire department in a Georgia community provides transportation to the prom in gleaming fire trucks, while a Morgan horse club in a rural New York area provides horse-drawn wagons for prom-goers to ride in. A Kentucky classic car club organizes a chauffeur service in antique automobiles that raises funds for worthy charities and provides a way for students to arrive at the prom in high style. In some communities parents with luxury cars dress up like chauffeurs and provide rides for large numbers of students. Imaginative transportation can make getting there half the fun. If there are no such programs in your community, maybe you can help organize a creative means of transport.

KEEPING IT AFFORDABLE

A group of high school boys got together and approached a tuxedo rental firm about a group rate for their prom tuxes. The result was a 15 percent discount. Hiring a chauffered limousine was too expensive for a group of friends going to the prom together, but they found out that an adult could rent a luxury car at the airport at a bargain weekend rate. One girl asked her uncle to rent the car and serve as chauffeur for the group. They went to the prom in style for about half the cost of a limousine.

Rick and Cathy were both on tight budgets, so they went to dinner before the prom at a restaurant that honored two-for-one coupons in a local entertainment book purchased by Rick's parents. Cathy saved on her gown by renting it from a theatrical-costume supplier. "I found a gorgeous forties-style cabaret gown. It was great-looking and different. I could have chosen from a sequined nightclub gown, a ruffled Southern belle's gown, or a medieval court dress. There were lots of possibilities."

Buying used, renting, or borrowing clothes are all ways to save money without sacrificing elegance and style. So are setting a budget and sticking with it, shopping carefully, sharing expenses, allowing enough time for prudent decision-making, planning your spending carefully, and resisting the temptation to spend above your limits. "Spending a lot doesn't guarantee quality, and spending a little doesn't mean that you don't get value. Spending wisely is what it's all about," cautions a business teacher who helps her students plan for their proms.

LEARNING TO DANCE

Many students already know how to dance, but a surprising number don't. And the ones who do aren't always sure of their ability at a formal dance. One way to overcome this potential problem is to learn as much as you can ahead of time. You can ask a parent or trusted adult to teach you. You can get together with friends and practice or you might take a series of lessons. Some schools offer dance instruction in physical education classes or in after-school programs. Private studios often have ballroom-dancing lessons, many in special "prom packages." Parent groups in some communities sponsor inexpensive or free classes for students planning to attend proms. Ask around. If there are no such programs in your school, perhaps you and a few friends can get something started.

DINING OUT

Sometimes, going to a dance or other school event means eating in a good restaurant before or afterward. Once again, planning and forethought are keys to a successful experience.

Before selecting a restaurant, ask your friends, parents, and other knowledgeable adults to recommend their favorite places. Some school librarians keep a file of menus from local restaurants. If your school doesn't have one, perhaps your librarian would be willing to start one. Visit the restaurant ahead of time and study the menu. If it seems affordable and you like the atmosphere and menu choices, book a reservation ahead of time. Remember to call and cancel the reservation if you change your plans.

You should know ahead of time how you plan to

*Dancing and dining are key
elements in the prom night fun.*

allocate expenses. If you are "going Dutch," with the boy and girl each paying for his or her own meal, decide in advance who will take the check and pay the cashier. If you are treating your date to dinner, say so up front. If you're not sure whether or not your date expects you to share in the cost, say so. If you don't feel you can afford a particular restaurant, don't be pressured by others into eating there. You won't enjoy yourself.

When you arrive at a restaurant, the host, headwaiter, or hostess will lead you to your seats. It's traditional etiquette for the girl to go ahead of her date and follow the host to the table. She should sit right down and allow the host to help slide in her chair. After that the boy takes his seat.

The waiter will then ask if you wish to order drinks. If you're going to the prom, you'll have to order soft drinks, coffee, tea, or other nonalcoholic beverages, even if either of you is over twenty-one, since most schools have rules barring attendance to anyone who has been drinking at all, regardless of age. Occasionally, bartenders will serve alcoholic beverages to minors, and you may know of places with a reputation for being "easy." Don't be tempted. You could get into trouble, face embarrassment, or be turned away at the prom. Most good restaurants offer nonalcoholic cocktails that you may choose.

You'll study the menu while you're having your drinks. When you've made up your mind what you want, fold your menu and set it aside so the waiter will know you are ready to order. In most restaurants the dinner selections include bread, potato, salads, and occasionally side dishes. Appetizers and desserts are rarely included, so be prepared for extra expense if you choose any. If you're not sure what's included with your meal, it's fine to ask.

When you are through, the waiter will bring the check to your table. The person who has planned to pay picks it up and looks it over to be sure the charges are accurate. If there are any questions, ask the waiter for an explanation. Most of the time, everything will be in order. In nice restaurants the procedure is usually to pay the waiter, so you put your money on top of the check and set it beside you where the waiter can see it. Your server will either take your check to the cashier and bring back the change or inform you that you're expected to pay the cashier directly as you leave.

After you've paid and you're ready to go, leave a tip on the table. Between 15 and 20 percent of the total bill before the tax is appropriate. If the service has been poor, however, you can reduce your tip to 10 percent and you can tip slightly more for extraordinarily good service.

ENJOYING YOUR BIG EVENING

When you arrive at the prom, you'll check your coat, sign in, or turn in your tickets and perhaps sign an agreement to stay drug and alcohol free. There may be a formal receiving line. This line may comprise the class officers, committee members, and other students who are serving in the capacity of hosts along with some adult advisers and chaperones. Go through the line and shake hands briefly with each person in it. If you know the person, say something pleasant. If you don't know the person, introduce yourself and your date. If you've brought someone from another school, introduce him or her as you go through the line. If there is no receiving line, greet the adults and committee members informally near the entrance. Don't worry about what is "correct" to do. Simply be polite and courteous and you'll do fine.

Now that you've arrived, checked in, and greeted others, the only thing to do for the rest of the evening is to relax and enjoy yourself. One way to enjoy yourself is to plan how you might deal with any problems that come up. "Students who think things through ahead of time have an easier time coping," says a school counselor.

The biggest single problem students say they have is how to face the issue of drinking. "I have friends who I know plan to drink. They can find ways. I may even have a couple of drinks myself," remarks one student.

So how do you deal with drinking problems that arise? First, recognize that you can only control your own behavior, and that you are not responsible for the behavior of others. Don't be pressured by others and don't try to exert direct pressure, either. Rather than lecture or preach, let your good example and your self-confidence influence your peers.

Second, steer clear of those you know might cause problems for you. Make your own decisions about what to do and not do. Stand up for yourself and stick with friends who either think like you do or respect your right to think for yourself. Define ahead of time the limits of your personal behavior. When you think things through, you'll feel more confident and you'll have a better time.

9

ASSEMBLIES, FAIRS, FESTIVALS, AND PAGEANTS

The same skills, techniques, and ideas used for planning proms are important for putting on other school programs such as assemblies, banquets, shows, and more sweeping events like carnivals, fairs, festivals, and pageants. All school programs have to be carefully planned. The same ingredients of a successful prom can go into other programs to make them successful, too.

The difference is scope. Some programs can be decided upon impulsively and organized in a day or less. Some can be entirely planned by students. Others require extensive coordination, long-range planning, and a lot of adult help. The idea is to mix and match ideas, themes, and plans to produce interesting school programs of almost endless variety.

Assemblies and awards banquets both offer programs usually limited to a specific purpose and relatively short time frame. Pageants and festivals are really a series of events that can be separately planned and coordinated by a central committee. Sometimes school classes, clubs, or groups participate in outside programs, such as community festivals. You'll use the same planning and people skills in greater or lesser degrees to participate in, plan for, or put on all types of programs. The idea isn't to replicate the good school programs described in this book, but to use the great ideas gathered here as a springboard for planning innovative programs that are just right for your school and to use the specific planning techniques to make your programs perfect.

ASSEMBLIES

A city high school in central Illinois has assembly programs that the entire student body awaits with pleasure. Many of the programs are planned by the students. A few are professional programs paid for by the parents' association or board of education and some are put on by administrators. Two assemblies are held each month on a regular basis and the planning is done far ahead of time.

Another Illinois high school holds assemblies sporadically. They always begin with the principal saying "a few" words. "A few thousand words is more like it," grumbles one student. By the time the program starts, the audience is already restless. Behavior is frequently a problem, so the administration is reluctant to allow students to get involved in planning the assemblies. There are no funds available to bring in interesting outside programs.

Assembly programs can have many different functions and are organized by different school groups. Some are put on strictly by the faculty and administration and are designed to provide information to students, conduct necessary school business, or prepare students to meet particular requirements.

Others are planned by the school's music or drama departments for concerts, plays, and student performances. Local organizations sometimes come in to provide programs for students. Still other assembly

GREAT IDEAS FOR ASSEMBLIES

Many of these assembly ideas belong in more than one category. Mix and match them to come up with an assembly program that's special and just right for the occasion you want to mark. You'll think of many more ideas as you go along.

AWARDS

Athletic
- Varsity Letter Presentation
- Celebration of a Winning Season
- Recognition of Team Accomplishment
- Athlete of the Week / Month / Year
- Presentation of Fitness / Health Awards

Academic
- Student of the Week / Month / Year
- Scholarship Presentations
- Announcing of Valedictorian / Salutatorian
- Honor Society Induction
- Departmental Honors (Music, English, Language, etc.)

Extra-curricular
- Announcement of Homecoming Court
- Student Government Elections
- Inauguration of Class Officers / Leaders

Adult
- Parent, Coach, Teacher, Leader of the Month / Year

Outside
- Legislator, Politician, Community Leader

Other
- Outstanding Organizations, Clubs, Groups

INFORMATION

This type of assembly can be put on whenever there is a need to convey information to the student body or to a particular group of students. Examples: — Testing preparation — College application process — Review or change of school rules — Introduction of school clubs and activities.

ENTERTAINMENT

- Plays and Skits
- Movies
- Musical Performances (student or professional)

EDUCATIONAL

Films, speakers, presentations, or shows on subjects studied by most students.

PROFESSIONAL

Assembly programs, to educate, and / or entertain, that are produced and staged by professional touring companies.

ORGANIZATIONAL

Programs staged or made available by community organizations and companies, such as health programs by an organization like the Heart Association or Cancer Society, or an energy program by a utility company.

INSPIRATIONAL

- Pep Rallies
- Victory Celebrations
- Motivational (Be Your Best!) Academic Programs
- Patriotic Programs
- Memorial Remembrance
- Honoring of Achievements

CEREMONIAL

- Coronation of Kings / Queens / Royal Courts
- Induction of Officers
- Presentation of Awards
- Memorial Services
- Patriotic Programs
- Moving Up, Class Day, Commencement, and other Rites of Passage
- Holiday Observances

programs are booked from among a large number of professional touring programs. These don't usually involve student planning.

Award assemblies, pep rallies, class meetings, student council-sponsored programs and assemblies held in conjunction with other events are often planned by students. Assemblies planned by student organizations are usually welcomed by school administrators. If your group has an idea for an assembly, chances are you'll find your principal willing to listen.

To put on a good assembly, you need to work within a precise framework. The schedule is important, since assemblies must fit into a tightly organized school day. For this reason, timing is vital. The planning tool to use is called a timed agenda. Every minute should be planned and participants fully informed of what they are expected to do, where they are supposed to be, and how long they will have to do it in.

Many assemblies staged by students or administrators are unnecessarily boring. Audiences may grow restless, and speakers may drone endlessly on. But this doesn't have to be the case. You can liven up assembly programs with variety, pacing, elements of entertainment, and freshness.

Assemblies are used to present awards, provide information, entertain, motivate, celebrate, give students public-speaking and performing experience, or serve a combination of purposes. Some of the most successful assemblies offer a variety of purposes to interest a broader spectrum of the student body.

"We have an all-purpose assembly at least once a month," says a school principal from Nevada. "Anything that comes up during the course of the month that might interest or inform the student body is scheduled for the assembly." Regular features of the Nevada school's assemblies are awards to the "Student of the Month" and "Teacher of the Month." The music department is always scheduled for a five- or ten-minute performance. Upcoming school events are previewed, if the planners wish. Speakers from outside the school with interesting or important messages are scheduled to make brief presentations. The result is a short, entertaining, and brisk program that students and faculty always enjoy.

A school in Louisiana holds a "This Is Your School" assembly every fall. All school clubs and organizations are invited to make brief presentations. The result is a lively program that gives needed exposure to worthwhile activities and imparts a lot of solid information to students about what is offered at the school.

Cheerleaders lead the applause for scholarship winners, and scholars in caps and gowns present athletic awards at assemblies in a San Francisco school noted for unusually interesting programs. "We like to mix and match our assembly programs," says the president of the student council.

To put on winning assemblies, remember to keep the pace brisk, interject variety, and hold shorter, more frequent assemblies. The idea is to leave students wishing for more, not wishing they were somewhere else.

PAGEANTS

Pageants are major events that contain a strong element of tradition, often mixed with competition, ritual, and ceremony. Pageants are traditionally held to select such individuals as homecoming kings and queens; winners of beauty, talent, and scholarship competitions; and representatives of groups and organizations such as ambassadors, princes, or princesses. Often, schools hold pageants to select their representatives in wider community contests.

An annual Thanksgiving weekend tradition in Charlotte, North Carolina, for example, is the Carolina

*Many pageants revolve around the theme
of royalty. Meet the Winter Queen (center),
flanked by two members of her court.*

Carousel. One of the highlights is the crowning of the
Carousel Queen, who then reigns over the parade and
major festival events. A number of high schools in the
area hold Carousel pageants where the school's Carousel Queen candidate is selected.

"I know that old-time beauty pageants have a bad name," says a teacher who runs the pageant in one high school. "But this can provide valuable experience for the kids. They seem to love it and we run our pageant as a fund-raiser. We've made a lot of money for other school projects by holding this pageant."

"The best aspect of pageants is meeting people whom you would have never met otherwise and gaining the ability to feel comfortable in front of people," says a student who won her high school pageant and went on to compete in the Carolina Carousel pageant.

Pageants don't have to be limited to the traditional. "We have a big pageant to select the student and teacher of the year," says the Nevada principal whose school holds monthly assemblies. The candidates are all the students and teachers of the month. They go through a series of competitions—some serious, some fun. "We invite judges from the school board, student body, and faculty as well as community leaders, professionals, representatives from area organizations, and politicians," says the principal. "It's a big deal and turns out to be a lot of fun."

Students compete in a public-speaking contest, a general-knowledge quiz, and a procession where they can either get dressed up or appear in costume. They are required to write an essay and be interviewed beforehand by panels of judges. They are given questions to answer extemporaneously on the big night. Teachers are put through a similar competition.

Basically, a pageant is a contest that's been organized to choose the recipient of a particular honor. Pageants are one way to choose homecoming kings and queens and the "royalty" for other festivals, such as a dairy princess, winter festival queen, or varsity king. Pageants can be staged during school assemblies or at evening programs. They can be serious and ceremonial or humorous. The format of most pageants includes the

GREAT IDEAS FOR PAGEANTS

CORONATION

- Homecoming King, Queen, Court
- Royalty for Special Dance or Banquet
- King, Queen or Royal Personage of a Festival
  Examples: King Bacchus of Mardi Gras
  Tulip Queen
  Reader Rex (Winner of Read-a-thon)

AWARD

- Teacher of the Year
- Student of the Week / Month / Year
- Mother, Father, Leader of the Year
- Athlete of the Week / Month / Year
- Honor Society Induction Ceremonies
- Politician Who Contributed to Education
- Presentation of Awards Established in Memory of an Individual
- Class Day Awards Program

INFORMATIONAL

- Cavalcade of Clubs (A program about school activities)
- Who's Who at School

CONTESTS

- Talent Show
- Popularity
- Spelling Bees
- Quiz Programs
- Battle of the Bands
- Mozart Flute Festival
- Beauty / Talent / Poise Contests (Miss America, Mr. Macho, etc.)
- Beautiful Baby
- Groovy Grandparents
- Superior Seniors
- Young and Talented
- Whiz Kids

*Girls competing for the honor
of being a festival queen kick up their
heels during a dance rehearsal.*

preliminary selection of contestants and then a series of competitive events that are judged by a panel of student leaders and adults. A typical queen pageant will have an evening-gown parade, talent competition, and brief question-and-answer period where contestants have an opportunity to demonstrate their poise and intelligence. Entertainment is sandwiched between the

115

competitive events. "Pageants sound difficult to put on, but actually they're quite easy to organize," says one teacher who helps with a pageant to select the homecoming queen in her school. "You have to plan carefully, but basically you can use a lot of different formats and give lots of students and teachers a chance to perform." If you have the cooperation of the various school departments, a pageant can be a great showcase for student talent. People enjoy attending pageants, too, which gives them terrific potential as fund-raising events.

FAIRS AND FESTIVALS

Fairs and festivals are a sweeping series of events organized around a particular theme. It may seem like an overwhelming job to organize a fair or a festival, but it doesn't need to be if you keep in mind that a festival is really a series of separate events. Each one can be planned by a separate committee, with a steering committee handling overall coordination. Breaking the job down into manageable chunks is the key to a successful festival.

Festivals, in fact, can be easier to organize than other events, because there's room for everyone's ideas and lots of innovation. Homecoming is a common and typical school festival that usually includes a variety of programs including an athletic competition, parade, pep assembly or rally, dance, queen pageant, dinner, and reception. Homecoming festivities often involve the entire community. Planners can toss in almost any good idea, such as a public-speaking contest, craft show, pot-luck fund-raiser, and competitions between teams formed from such groups as teachers, firefighters, and government bodies. School classes and organizations can compete in decorating floats or raising money for their treasuries or worthy causes. Related school events can be easy to plan and fun to participate in. In many schools, each day of homecoming week has

Top: *Homecoming usually centers around an athletic event. A parade can include a float-decorating competition.*
Bottom: *The coronation of a king and queen is often a homecoming highlight.*

GREAT IDEAS FOR FAIRS
AND FESTIVALS

Although fairs and festivals are major events with broad overall themes, they usually have a number of smaller events associated with them. Fairs, fetes, and bazaars are often sales-oriented with a series of booths offering items for sale such as food, preserves, craft items, and souvenirs. Fairs may also offer games and programs.
Festivals are generally a series of events organized around a single theme and may take place over a fairly extended period of time.
Some fairs and festivals will take place entirely within a school. Others are community-wide events in which school groups participate. Start your planning by selecting a theme or reason for the fair or festival, then plan events which would fit with the theme.

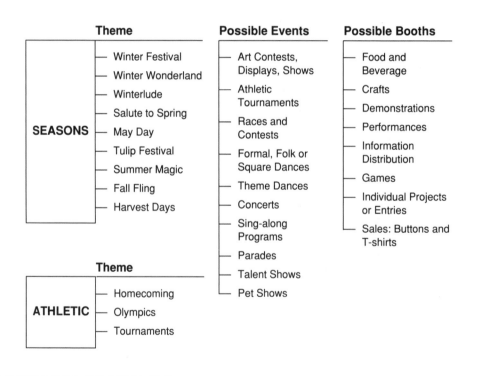

Theme	Possible Events	Possible Booths
SEASONS — Winter Festival — Winter Wonderland — Winterlude — Salute to Spring — May Day — Tulip Festival — Summer Magic — Fall Fling — Harvest Days	— Art Contests, Displays, Shows — Athletic Tournaments — Races and Contests — Formal, Folk or Square Dances — Theme Dances — Concerts — Sing-along Programs — Parades — Talent Shows — Pet Shows	— Food and Beverage — Crafts — Demonstrations — Performances — Information Distribution — Games — Individual Projects or Entries — Sales: Buttons and T-shirts

Theme

ATHLETIC — Homecoming
— Olympics
— Tournaments

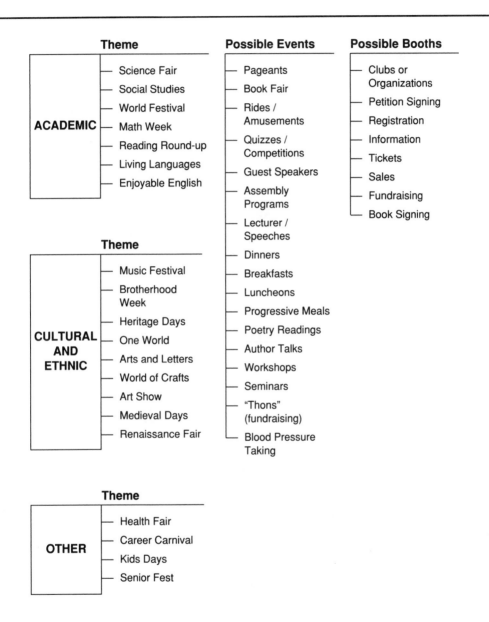

Theme

ACADEMIC
- Science Fair
- Social Studies
- World Festival
- Math Week
- Reading Round-up
- Living Languages
- Enjoyable English

Theme

CULTURAL AND ETHNIC
- Music Festival
- Brotherhood Week
- Heritage Days
- One World
- Arts and Letters
- World of Crafts
- Art Show
- Medieval Days
- Renaissance Fair

Theme

OTHER
- Health Fair
- Career Carnival
- Kids Days
- Senior Fest

Possible Events
- Pageants
- Book Fair
- Rides / Amusements
- Quizzes / Competitions
- Guest Speakers
- Assembly Programs
- Lecturer / Speeches
- Dinners
- Breakfasts
- Luncheons
- Progressive Meals
- Poetry Readings
- Author Talks
- Workshops
- Seminars
- "Thons" (fundraising)
- Blood Pressure Taking

Possible Booths
- Clubs or Organizations
- Petition Signing
- Registration
- Information
- Tickets
- Sales
- Fundraising
- Book Signing

a special theme or plan for clothing and activities, such as school-colors day, dress-up day, "Hats off to Majors" (when everyone wears silly hats), backwards day, or "Sock It To 'Em Day" (where dippy socks are high fashion).

Other fairs, festivals, carnivals, and cavalcades can be organized around such themes as health, careers, and seasons, or can be used to promote arts and ideas, such as craft shows, art festivals, and book fairs. Academic subjects lend themselves to festivals, too. Foreign Language Week is a big event at one school, with a wide variety of food and cultural demonstrations. Other ideas include Social Studies Week, You Are What You Eat Week (planned around the subject of nutrition), and Teacher Recognition Week. Festival events can include displays, demonstrations, sales, parades, booths, performances, dances, banquets, assemblies, contests, games, and novelty events.

"This is the place to be as open to ideas as possible and to welcome all segments of the student body and the wider community," says the organizer of her community's annual winter carnival. "We have a queen pageant, booths set up all over the community, dances, dinners, shows, a snow-sculpture contest, and demonstrations of everything from the latest firefighting equipment to quilting techniques. Anyone with a good idea is welcome to participate and to organize yet another contest, show, or display. The winter festival keeps growing. It's a major community event."

Festivals offer the opportunity to plan and participate at all levels. Your group can limit your efforts to organizing a single booth or modest event, or you can get involved on the steering committee. A good way to get practical leadership experience, raise funds, and have fun is to participate with a group from your school in an outside event. "This is the best of both worlds," says a girl who organized a popcorn stand for her chess club at the winter carnival. "We're making money for our club, having a great time, and meeting all kinds of interesting people."

School groups can operate games of skill or chance, sell items at booths, put on performances, pass out information, hold demonstrations, compete in contests, and provide specialty services such as ushering. Festivals and fairs offer opportunities to participate at many different levels of involvement. The next time you hear about a community festival, think of ways in which you and your school group might participate.

Planning fairs, festivals, and carnivals isn't hard if you start early, stay flexible, welcome ideas, and keep events open to as wide a cross-section of the community as possible. The most successful events grow and evolve each year until they become well-entrenched community traditions.

10
PUTTING IT ALL TOGETHER

This book is a mixture of general guidelines for planning good programs and specific ideas to help you. It doesn't offer an exact "recipe" for any single prom, pageant, or program. Rather, it's designed to help you get started and identify tools and techniques you'll find useful during the process of planning perfect proms, programs, and pageants.

General planning skills will be useful to you in putting on all types of programs. Specific types of programs mean special challenges, but the same underlying philosophy of planning ahead, breaking the overall job down into its component parts, delegating responsibility for component parts to specific committees or individuals, communicating clearly, working well with others, and remembering to wrap up loose ends after the program is over will serve you well.

DEVELOPING A MASTER CHECKLIST

In order to plan your specific event, develop a master checklist to help organize your ideas and identify areas where committees or individuals need to make plans and decisions. Here is a sample checklist that you may want to adapt for your school program. Possible decisions for a prom are in *italics*.

BASIC INFORMATION

- NAME OF EVENT
  This can be general, specific, or both.
  Annual Junior/Senior Prom—"A Night to Remember."

- TYPE OF EVENT
  Formal dance

- PRIMARY SPONSORS OR ORGANIZERS
  Traditionally given annually by the junior class for the senior class.

- THEME OR POSSIBLE THEMES
  "It Happened One Night," "A Little Night Music," "Magic Night," "A Night to Remember."

- PURPOSE(S)
  List as many reasons as you can think of for putting on and/or attending this program.
  Having fun, gaining experience, learning new skills, providing entertainment, continuing a long-standing tradition, preparing for adulthood.

- DATE(S)
  Be sure your choice of date doesn't conflict with competing events, athletic practices or competitions, or test and exam schedules. Try to allow for backup dates. List alternatives.
  Saturday, June 23, 1996. Date set in advance by board of education as part of official school calendar.

- LOCATION
  Regency Hotel, Ballroom A

PRELIMINARY TIMETABLE

List the date on which you must get started with the early planning and a series of intermediate dates at which certain tasks need to be accomplished.

Date and location have already been set by the school administration. Student planning schedule:

September, 1993. First organizational meeting held with class officers (class of 1997 and 1996) and class advisers and interested class members attracted by announcements and posters. Meeting should include brainstorming for themes, identification of committees that will be eventually needed, and election of chair.

1st Semester, 1993–94. Recruiting of committee chairs and members.

2nd Semester, 1994. Committees set up, staffed, and starting to meet regularly.

September, 1995. Progress meeting of all committees and adviser.

January, 1996. Final planning stage begins. All committees should be fully functioning and specific tasks identified. Each committee should now have a timetable of its own with dates identified for completion of tasks.

COMMITTEES NEEDED

Steering Committee of class officers, adviser, and early volunteers. *This committee will make or approve major decisions, clear decisions with administrators and coordinate the activities and decisions of other committees.*

Decorations

1. Plan decorations for ballroom, lobby, tables, walls, ceiling, entrances, and other necessary areas.

2. Secure necessary items for making decorations.

3. Set up work sessions to do the actual decorating. Start in the fall for such things as making centerpieces and banners. Schedule plenty of work time at the hotel the week before.

4. *Coordinate with other committees.*

5. *Make sure decorations get cleaned up afterward.*

Food. *Deal with the hotel in selecting a refreshment menu that falls within the budget. Take adviser to all meetings with hotel personnel. Collect menus from area restaurants for a school library resource.*

Favors/Photos. *Work with adviser to decide on information to be printed in the prom program and souvenir booklet. Decide on other favors to be provided to those who attend. Arrange for professional couple-portrait photography. Select gifts for chaperones and advisers. Coordinate with budget committee, decorations committee, entertainment committee, and ticket committee. Arrange for videotaping by your school's audiovisual department and coverage by yearbook and school paper photographers.*

Tickets/Invitations. *Arrange for printing and sending of invitations to each senior. Work with budget committee to establish ticket prices. Obtain souvenir tickets, possibly keychains. Have prom rules printed on an individual contract for each student to sign on arrival.*

Music. *With help of sponsor, line up live band and/or sound system. Look for volunteer musicians to offer brief alternatives during band breaks. Coordinate with budget committee and entertainment committee.*

Entertainment. *Plan the program for the evening in detail. Produce the timed agenda for the evening (in coordination with the steering committee). Line up an emcee and other entertainment elements. Plan specialty dances, coronation, grand march, etc.*

Publicity. *Send out press releases as requested by other committees in order to recruit volunteers, obtain donations, create goodwill, and publicize prom rules. Help out with printed programs. Help with announcements, posters, and other communication items. Work closely with class adviser and steering committee.*

Transportation. *Gather information on limousine services, car rentals, luxury buses, school buses, hay wagons,* and fire trucks. Work with principal, parent adviser(s), and board of education to develop transportation rules. The board of education has ruled that school buses will have to be used if the prom is held in a hotel, but the principal says the board might change its mind if we can come up with a safe and economical alternate method of transportation.

Election. *Oversee the choosing of the prom king and queen and plan for the specifics of the coronation. There have been problems with this at other proms, so the principal has suggested this special committee to find a fair way to handle the selection and crowning of the king and queen. This committee will also probably decide who will be honored in the opening promenade (grand march).*

Mop-up. *Make sure the hotel ballroom is cleaned up and that all borrowed items are returned. Oversee and coordinate the writing of thank-you notes and follow-up publicity, and make sure each committee files a final report and takes care of its own final details. Coordinate with the steering committee and all other committees. Oversee the formal evaluation process. This committee is also the suggestion of the principal, who says follow-up has sometimes been neglected in the past.*

LEADERSHIP POSITIONS

Overall Chair. *Probably should be chosen early from the preliminary steering committee. Could be a class officer, but doesn't have to be. Chair will work closely with adviser and coordinate the efforts of all committees.*

Steering Committee Members. *At first these will be the only people working on the plans and they'll all work together. As specific jobs and duties are identified, many of these people will be elected or appointed as committee chairs.*

Committee Chairs. *Gradually, chairs for each committee will be named. Each committee chair will recruit members of the committee and be responsible for reporting back to the general chair, steering committee, class adviser, and principal.*

126

ADULT HELP NEEDED

Principal. *Whether we want it or not, the principal is taking an active role in the planning of our prom because of problems in the past. We have to get all major decisions approved by him and we have to get any contracts signed by him.*

Class Adviser. *Our class adviser will work with the steering committee and overall chair. She'll be available to committee chairs and committee members, too, for advice and suggestions.*

Parents. *We need parents to help us, especially in the area of transportation. We also need parents to organize an all-night party if we can find a group willing to do this.*

BUDGET NOTES

The class officers have already decided that half of all class funds raised will be used for the prom. The PTA has promised a contribution of $500 and the Kiwanis Club has offered a grant of $200 to help make our prom drug and alcohol free. The rest of the money will have come from ticket sales. In the past, seniors have not been charged unless they bring a date from a different school. Juniors have paid to attend, since they are the hosts. The principal says it may be necessary this year to have seniors pay, too, since we are having the prom at a hotel. Still under discussion is whether or not to have the hotel provide dinner or just to have cold drinks and light refreshments. This will affect the ticket prices.

SOURCES OF INFORMATION, IDEAS, AND HELP

Each committee should start a source list. Ask at the library for books, pamphlets, and other information. Get names of catalogue companies from Athletic Department.

FOLLOW-UP

(See notes on mop-up committee.)

OTHER NOTES AND IDEAS

Should we try to find a parent to be a permanent part of the steering committee? Some kids think this is a good idea but others think parents can be difficult. We'll have to work this out.

Another important thing to do early is to meet with the principal and class adviser to work out what rules, regulations, and practices the student planners will have to follow.

There have been complaints about costs in the past. Can we find ways to save money, both for committees and individuals?

This checklist isn't designed to be filled in all at once, nor is it designed to be comprehensive. Work on it as you go and adapt it to your program. You might want to add some categories and delete others. That's fine. In fact, your ability to adapt this checklist to meet your school's specific needs is one of the vital plan ning skills that will help you succeed.

11

GREAT IDEAS
FROM ALL OVER

The audience was hushed. The nine other finalists watched intently as the candidate for Mother of the Year, who was dressed in a police uniform, considered her answer to the question that had been posed by the judges: "What is the biggest problem facing mothers today?" She glanced at the ceiling, then out across the footlights toward the sea of faces that formed the nearly silent audience. Finally, she gave her one-word answer.

"Kids," she said in a strong, clear voice.

The audience broke into laughter and applause. The judges smiled. Even the other contestants had to smile.

The police mother won. The audience loved it, the contestants had a good time, and the pageant raised hundreds of dollars for the student council treasury and an equal amount for the winning mother's favorite charity.

This wildly successful "Mother of the Year" program was hatched when a school group from upstate New York wanted to hold a fund-raiser and decided to put on a pageant. The only free date was the Saturday night before Mother's Day. That gave them an idea— why not hold a pageant to find the best mother in town?

"We used the format of the Miss America Pageant, except our contestants were local mothers who had been nominated by their kids, husbands, or friends," says one of the student organizers. "Instead of an evening-gown competition, we had a costume parade where the mothers dressed in a way that symbolized motherhood to them. We had witches, angels, a dancing can of spinach, a broken record, a police officer, a referee, a drill sergeant, and a wild-animal tamer."

This popular pageant used an old idea with a creative twist, a fresh variation on a favorite theme. You, too, can bring freshness to your school events by using some of the ideas shared in this book and by applying your own creativity. Here are some more great ideas from all over to get your imagination going.

Michigan seniors decided to stretch out the fun of their prom night, get more wear out of their dresses, and provide a valuable community service as well by holding a really "senior" prom and inviting local senior citizens to attend a special prom in their honor at the school. This prom with a twist generated national publicity, a lot of good feelings, and a great time for everyone. "I had more fun here than at my own prom," said one high school student. Now the Senior Citizens' Prom is an annual event to which the entire student body and community look forward.

Several communities in Massachusetts hold a joint sale of used prom gowns and accessories every year. Gowns from one school are sold at a different school so that students don't have to worry about showing up at their prom in one of their classmate's old gowns. Organizers invite a cosmetologist to provide hair and makeup consultations and a seamstress to advise about alterations.

This young man escorts his "date" to a Senior Citizens Prom in Michigan. The event, now a popular annual tradition planned by the students, affords both young and old generations a chance to mingle in a special way.

The Pageant of Bands has become an annual ritual for a community in the Northeast. What started out many years ago as a small school-band competition has grown into a community celebration with a parade, concerts, and contests spread out over a three-day period. "This pageant has a sound educational and musical purpose, but it goes well beyond that," says the musical director of the host school. "This has to be one of the best parades imaginable. Just imagine the impact of not one or two but dozens of marching bands."

A home economics class and its teacher decided to devote a series of class sessions to planning for the prom. When students began their research, they could find no books on the subject, so they decided to put together their own prom-survival guide. They surveyed fellow students and gathered information on student opinions and ideas. They studied and discussed budgets, shopping methods, etiquette, and other prom-attendance skills. Then they put their observations together into a booklet. Their teacher sent the booklet to *Scholastic Choices* magazine, which published a series of articles based on the students' research and tips (see Periodicals under Bibliography.)

The board of education in one community banned private transportation to the prom when a traffic accident caused by a young drunken driver claimed the lives of seven students. Those who wanted to go to the prom would have to ride in school buses, the board decreed. A group of parents and teachers, wanting to take the sting out of the board's decision, rented chauffeurs' uniforms for the bus drivers and decorated the buses with banners, flowers, and streamers. They arranged a motorcade from the school to the prom, complete with a police escort. When the buses pulled up to the hotel where the prom was being held, students were welcomed by searchlights crisscrossing the sky. As each couple stepped off the bus, their names were announced by the principal, who was dressed up like a hotel doorman.

The principal of an Ohio school started an informal dating service by pairing up students who wanted prom dates but hadn't found them with each other. At another school, all students were encouraged to attend the prom, even without dates. "Lots of kids came in groups," says the committee chair. "There were novelty dances and special events to get people mixing. The kids without dates seemed to have just as good a time as the kids who were paired off from the beginning."

The Honor Society in one school offered a "rent-a-date" service to students at other schools located nearby but not in the same community. All of the paid dates were carefully screened honor students who donated the proceeds to their class treasury.

One senior class selected a class song during the freshman year and continued to use it during the four years of high school. Naturally, the special song was a poignant last dance at the senior prom. A music teacher at another school arranged a slow dance version of the school fight song for the band to play at the homecoming dance. The "fight dance" was such a hit that it became a standard at all school dances. The school concert band taped a version for use with sound systems and a rock 'n' roll arrangement soon followed.

All of these great ideas are yours for the taking, needing only your committee's fresh approach or your group's new twist to translate them into successful affairs just right for your school. Good luck with putting on your perfect prom, program, or pageant!

GLOSSARY

Agenda—a list of items to be covered at a meeting.

Baccalaureate—a speech or sermon delivered to graduates at commencement ceremonies or at a special get-together for the purpose, often a breakfast, luncheon, or banquet. Usually, but not always, a separate event from commencement.

Brainstorming—a creative, idea-generating session first developed by advertising agencies to come up with fresh advertising concepts. According to brainstorming's ground rules, every idea is written down and none are scoffed at. The idea is to generate as many ideas as possible in a short time in the hope that some will take root or inspire other ideas.

Break-even Point—the point at which projected income and outgo are the same. After the break-even point a program or project begins to show a profit. The break-even point can be calculated on the basis of attendance figures, ticket sales, or contributions received.

Budget—a financial plan that lists project income and expenses. A balanced budget is one where income and expenses equal the same amount. A deficit budget is one where income is less than spending and a surplus budget is one where income exceeds expenses.

Cavalcade—a term that comes from the Latin for "to go on horseback." It used to mean a horseback procession, but its meaning has expanded to include a procession, parade, or pageant.

Chair, Chairman, Chairperson, Chairwoman—the head of a committee. This person used to be called a chairman, but is more frequently called simply a chair or chairperson in order to avoid sexist language.

Cooperative Extension Service—the local, grassroots, or county arm of the federal land grant university system. The purpose of the Cooperative Extension Service is to disseminate practical research information from the universities into the communities. There is a designated land grant university in every state that provides information through county extension services. Cooperative extension agents provide useful information and programs on cooking, textiles, decorating, agriculture, gardening, landscaping, environment, leadership, and other practical subjects; and run training sessions on a variety of topics.

Committee—the basic element of most planning organizations; a group of people elected or appointed to perform specific tasks or accomplish specific goals. Committees usually have specialized functions.

Contingency Fund—extra money in a budget that is set aside to be used for emergencies and unanticipated expenses at a chair's discretion.

Contingency Plan—a backup plan that will allow an event to continue or be held under different circumstances in case of adverse weather, unforeseen changes, and other contingencies.

Cotillion—a dance with complicated steps and much changing of partners. Sometimes a society dance with elaborate associated rituals and proscribed behavior. A predecessor of the modern prom.

Debutante Ball—a formal dance where a young woman, a debutante, is officially presented to society or where the season's debutantes are honored. A rite of passage and predecessor of the modern prom.

Delegate—as a verb, delegate means to entrust the care or management of something to another person or group. As a noun, a delegate is a representative, someone empowered or authorized to act on behalf of another individual or group.

Dutch Treat—dividing expenses between the boy and girl on a date or having each member of a group pay for his or her own expenses.

Etiquette—a formal framework of polite conduct that smooths social relations and insures continuance of traditions by prescribing good manners and common-sense rules of behavior.

Evaluation—part of the planning process where opinions of those involved in an event are officially solicited, reports are made, and the program analyzed with a view to making improvements for the next time.

Fair—a gathering of people to buy, sell, display, and celebrate.

Festival—a series of related events, such as assemblies, demonstrations, programs, parties, dinners, parades, and games, that are organized around a common theme.

Fiscal—having to do with money; financial.

Formal—ceremonial, traditional, and dressy. Formal dress usually dictates tuxedos for men and gowns for women, either full-length or very dressy. Formal occasions are those where behavior and dress are prescribed to fit with certain form and custom. Most school proms are formal.

Ground Rules—rules for making decisions that are agreed to in advance by the planners. A committee might agree, for example, that discussions will be limited in length and that all decisions will be formally voted upon with a simple majority of the committee members present sufficient to approve the decision.

Inverted Pyramid—a journalistic style of writing so designed that the first paragraph is capable of standing alone if an article needs be cut. Information is included in declining order of importance.

Meeting—a session where people get together to make plans, reach decisions, hold discussions, or conduct business. The meeting is a vital planning tool.

Motif—a salient, dominant, or frequently repeated feature of an event, work of art, or musical piece.

Pageant—pageants evolved from public entertainments that represent scenes from history and legend. They are rich in tradition, ritual, and significance and have evolved into modern contests to select beauty queens and others being honored with ceremonial titles and awards. Many pageants have themes of royalty.

Parliamentary Procedure—a formal method of running meetings, usually not necessary for school planning committees.

Press Release—a concise news story that is sent to newspapers and other media outlets. Most press releases are tightly focused, short, and written in the inverted pyramid style where the first paragraph contains most of the essential information.

Pro tem—from the Latin meaning "for the time being." Term used to describe a temporary committee or situation.

Prom—a formal school dance, usually given especially for the senior and/or junior class. The word prom evolved from promenade, the opening march of a formal society dance.

Public Service Announcement—a free promotional announcement on radio or television.

Publicity—distribution of information about a school event through the media and use of posters, handbills, and other methods. Not to be confused with paid advertising.

Receiving Line—a formal greeting system where hosts, hostesses, and dignitaries line up to meet everyone arriving at an event. Proms sometimes have receiving lines where members of the planning committee, class advisers, student officials, and others line up to greet arriving prom guests.

Semiformal—a dressy event, usually a dinner or dance, requiring males to wear suits and females to wear short party dresses.

Steering Committee—a coordinating or supervising committee responsible for organizing and overseeing a particular event or series of events.

Subcommittee—a committee that is formed by another to handle a more specialized function related to the primary committee's area of responsibility.

Survey—a useful tool to gather information for decision-making, solicit opinions, recruit volunteers, and obtain data. Surveys can be informal or scientific, written or verbal. For an informal survey, planners might just ask a few representative individuals what they think of an idea. A detailed written questionnaire sent to a large number of individuals with the results tabulated and analyzed is a more formal survey technique.

Tea Dance—an afternoon dance that was a predecessor of the modern prom.

Theme—the major subject or focus of an artwork, musical composition, or event. A unifying thread that is woven throughout the tapestry of an event. A central background idea that becomes the basis for the selection of music, decor, colors, and other elements of a school event.

Timed Agenda—a minute-by-minute schedule of a meeting or event. The timed agenda is a vital planning tool for most school programs and should be carefully developed, tested, and followed.

BIBLIOGRAPHY

Periodicals

"Are You Prom Prepared?" *Teen*, March 1990, 94.

Hubbard, Kim, with Azizian, Carol. "A High School in Michigan Holds a Really Senior Prom." *People Weekly*, June 13, 1988, 132–3.

"License to Thrill, the Most Prom-Pretty Dresses." *Seventeen*, March 1990, 228–50.

Price, Bonni. "17 Boffo Things to Do on Prom Night (Instead of Going to the Prom)." *Seventeen*, May 1987, 172–3.

"Prom Survival Guide." *Scholastic Choices*, March 1990, 6–13.

Your Prom. Published by *Modern Bride*. Spring 1990.

Other Resources

The following businesses publish free or inexpensive catalogues of supplies and useful planning guides. Most will send catalogues and helpful information on request:

Anderson's:
4875 White Bear Parkway
White Bear Lake, MN 55110
(800) 328-9640
School Events Catalogue, Prom
and Party Catalogue, School Spirit
Catalogue, Post-Prom and Graduation
Party Catalogue, Anderson's Prom
Planning Manual, Anderson's Post-
Prom and Graduation Party Planning Manual

Columbus Manufacturer's Inc.
P.O. Box 423
Columbus, MS 39701
(800) 647-1056
School Promotions Catalogue

Creative Promotions
P.O. Box 10833, St. Paul, MN 55110
(800) 642-1081
Creative Promotions Fund-raising Catalogue

Oriental Trading Company
4206 South 108th Street
Omaha, NE 68137-1215
(402) 331-1511

U.S. Toy Company
1227 E. 119th Street
Grandview, MO 60430
(800) 255-6124
Carnival, Decoration and Party Catalogue
and *Carnival Planning Guide for*
Successful Fund-Raising Events

Wincraft Incorporated
1205 East Sanborn St.
P.O. Box 888, Winona, MN 55987
(800) 533-8100
Spirit Leader's Catalogue

INDEX

142